Illumine My World

Illumine My World

Bahá'í Prayers and Meditations for Peace

Compiled by Bahá'í Publishing

Bahá'í
PUBLISHING
Wilmette, Illinois

Bahá'í Publishing
415 Linden Avenue, Wilmette, Illinois 60091-2844

Printed in the United States of America on acid-free paper ∞

12 11 10 09 4 3 2 1

Library of Congress Cataloging-in-Publication Data
Illumine my world : Bahá'í prayers and meditations for peace / compiled by Bahá'í Publishing.
p. cm.
Includes bibliographical references and index.
ISBN 978-1-931847-65-0 (alk. paper)
1. Bahai Faith—Prayers and devotions. 2. Peace—Religious aspects—Bahai Faith. I. Bahá'u'lláh, 1817-1892. II. Bab, 'Ali Muhammad Shirazi, 1819-1850. III. 'Abdu'l-Bahá, 1844-1921. IV. Bahá'í Publishing Trust.
BP360.I46 2009
297.9'3433—dc22
2009023092

Cover design by Misha Maynerick
Book design by Patrick Falso

Contents

Introduction 1

I. A Statement of the Universal House of Justice, October 1985 3

II. Prayers and Writings 39

Aid and Assistance 41

America 47

Children 49

For the Departed 57

Evening 63

Family 67

Healing 71

For Women 80

For Infants 82

The Long Healing Prayer 84

Humanity 91

Marriage 99

Morning 107

Protection 115
Tests and Difficulties 133
Unity 147
Women 151
Expectant Mothers 165
Youth 167
III. Selections from the Writings of
Bahá'u'lláh and 'Abdu'l-Bahá 175
Tablet of Aḥmad 177
Fire Tablet 181
Tablet of the Holy Mariner 189
Tablets of Visitation 199
Bahá'u'lláh and the Báb 200
'Abdu'l-Bahá 204
Tablet of Carme 207
Tablet of Wisdom 213
Words of Wisdom 237
Notes 241
References 247
Index of First Lines 249

Introduction

Illumine My World is the latest compilation of Bahá'í writings that addresses key issues in the world today and offers comfort to the overwhelmed reader. As the global fabric that knits our planet together continues to unravel, the reader can find within these pages the love and reassurance of Bahá'u'lláh, the Prophet-Founder of the Bahá'í Faith; His forerunner the Báb; and His son 'Abdu'l-Bahá.

The Bahá'í Faith is an independent world religion that began in 1844 in Persia (present-day Iran). Since its inception, the Bahá'í Faith has spread to 235 nations and territories and has been accepted by more than five million people. Bahá'ís believe that there is only one God, that all the major world religions come from God, and that all the members of the human race are essentially members of one family. Bahá'ís strive to eliminate all forms of prejudice and believe that people of all races, nations, social status, and religious backgrounds are equal in the sight of God. The Bahá'í Faith also teaches that each individual is responsible for the independent investigation of truth, that science and religion are in harmony, and that men and women are equal in the sight of God.

The current volume is divided into three sections. The first section contains a letter written in 1985 from the Universal House of Justice, the governing body of the Bahá'í Faith, to the people of the world. The second section is composed of prayers and writings of Bahá'u'lláh, the Báb, and 'Abdu'l-Bahá, as well as selections from utterances by 'Abdu'l-Bahá. The third and final section contains longer selections from the writings of Bahá'u'lláh and 'Abdu'l-Bahá, some of which are being made available to a general audience for the first time.

All parts of this book address, in one form or another, topics that are essential for the happiness of the individual as well as that of our global society. It is hoped that the writings within these pages will provide a sense of peace and security to the reader who is longing for a refuge in our world today.

I

A STATEMENT OF THE UNIVERSAL HOUSE OF JUSTICE, OCTOBER 1985

To the Peoples of the World: The Great Peace towards which people of goodwill throughout the centuries have inclined their hearts, of which seers and poets for countless generations have expressed their vision, and for which from age to age the sacred scriptures of mankind have constantly held the promise, is now at long last within the reach of the nations. For the first time in history it is possible for everyone to view the entire planet, with all its myriad diversified peoples, in one perspective. World peace is not only possible but inevitable. It is the next stage in the evolution of this planet—in the words of one great thinker, "the planetization of mankind."

Whether peace is to be reached only after unimaginable horrors precipitated by humanity's stubborn clinging to old patterns of behavior, or is to be embraced now by an act of consultative will, is the choice before all who inhabit the earth. At this critical juncture when the intractable problems confronting nations have been fused into one common concern for the whole world, failure to stem the tide of conflict and disorder would be unconscionably irresponsible.

Among the favorable signs are the steadily growing strength of the steps towards world order taken initially near the beginning of this century in the creation of the League of Nations, succeeded by the more broadly based United Nations Organization; the achievement since the Second World War of independence by the majority of all the nations on earth, indicating the completion of the process of nation building, and the involvement of these fledgling nations with older ones in matters of mutual concern; the consequent vast increase in cooperation among hitherto isolated and antagonistic peoples and groups in international undertakings in the scientific, educational, legal, economic and cultural fields; the rise in recent decades of an unprecedented number of international humanitarian organizations; the spread of women's and youth movements calling for an end to war; and the spontaneous spawning of widening networks of ordinary people seeking understanding through personal communication.

The scientific and technological advances occurring in this unusually blessed century portend a great surge forward in the social evolution of the planet and indicate the means by which the practical problems of humanity may be solved. They provide, indeed, the very means for the administration of the complex life of a united world. Yet barriers persist. Doubts, misconceptions, prejudices, suspicions and narrow self-interest beset nations and peoples in their relations one to another.

It is out of a deep sense of spiritual and moral duty that we are impelled at this opportune moment to invite your attention to the penetrating insights first communicated to the rulers of mankind more than a century ago by Bahá'u'lláh, Founder of the Bahá'í Faith, of which we are the Trustees.

"The winds of despair," Bahá'u'lláh wrote, "are, alas, blowing from every direction, and the strife that divides and afflicts the human race is daily increasing. The signs of impending convulsions and chaos can now be discerned, inasmuch as the prevailing order appears to be lamentably defective." This prophetic judgment has been amply confirmed by the common experience of humanity. Flaws in the prevailing order are conspicuous in the inability of sovereign states organized as United Nations to exorcise the specter of war, the threatened collapse of the international economic order, the spread of anarchy and terrorism, and the intense suffering which these and other afflictions are causing to increasing millions. Indeed, so much have aggression and conflict come to characterize our social, economic and religious systems, that many have succumbed to the view that such behavior is intrinsic to human nature and therefore ineradicable.

With the entrenchment of this view, a paralyzing contradiction has developed in human affairs. On the one hand, people of all nations proclaim not only their readiness but their longing for peace and harmony, for an end to the harrowing apprehensions tormenting their daily lives. On the other, uncritical assent is given to the proposition that human beings are incorrigibly selfish and aggressive and thus incapable of erecting a social system at once progressive and peaceful, dynamic and harmonious, a system giving free play to individual creativity and initiative but based on cooperation and reciprocity.

As the need for peace becomes more urgent, this fundamental contradiction, which hinders its realization, demands a reassessment of the assumptions upon which the commonly held view of mankind's historical predicament is based. Dispassionately examined, the evidence reveals that such conduct, far from expressing man's true self, represents a distortion of the human spirit. Satisfaction on this point will enable all people to set in motion constructive social forces which, because they are consistent with human nature, will encourage harmony and cooperation instead of war and conflict.

To choose such a course is not to deny humanity's past but to understand it. The Bahá'í Faith regards the current world confusion and calamitous condition in human affairs as a natural phase in an organic process leading ultimately and irresistibly to the unification of the human race in a single social order whose boundaries are those of the planet. The human race, as a distinct, organic unit, has passed through evolutionary stages analogous to the stages of infancy and childhood in the lives of its individual members, and is now in the culminating period of its turbulent adolescence approaching its long-awaited coming of age.

A candid acknowledgment that prejudice, war and exploitation have been the expression of immature stages in a vast historical process and that the human race is today experiencing the unavoidable tumult which marks its collective coming of age is not a reason for despair but a prerequisite to undertaking the stupendous enterprise of building a peaceful world. That such an enterprise is possible, that the necessary constructive forces do exist, that unifying social structures can be erected, is the theme we urge you to examine.

Whatever suffering and turmoil the years immediately ahead may hold, however dark the immediate circumstances, the Bahá'í community believes that humanity can confront this supreme trial with confidence in its ultimate outcome. Far from signalizing the end of civilization, the convulsive changes towards which humanity is being ever more rapidly impelled will serve to release the "potentialities inherent in the station of man" and reveal "the full measure of his destiny on earth, the innate excellence of his reality."

I

The endowments which distinguish the human race from all other forms of life are summed up in what is known as the human spirit; the mind is its essential quality. These endowments have enabled humanity to build civilizations and to prosper materially. But such accomplishments alone have never satisfied the human spirit, whose mysterious nature inclines it towards transcendence, a reaching towards an invisible realm, towards the ultimate reality, that unknowable essence of essences called God. The religions brought to mankind by a succession of spiritual luminaries have been the primary link between humanity and that ultimate reality, and have galvanized and refined mankind's capacity to achieve spiritual success together with social progress.

No serious attempt to set human affairs aright, to achieve world peace, can ignore religion. Man's perception and practice of it are largely the stuff of history. An eminent historian described religion as a "faculty of human nature." That the perversion of this faculty has contributed to much of the confusion in society and the conflicts in and between individuals can hardly be denied. But neither can any fair-minded observer discount the preponderating influence exerted by religion on the vital expressions of civilization. Furthermore, its indispensability to social order has repeatedly been demonstrated by its direct effect on laws and morality.

Writing of religion as a social force, Bahá'u'lláh said: "Religion is the greatest of all means for the establishment of order in the world and for the peaceful contentment of all that dwell therein." Referring to the eclipse or corruption of religion, he wrote: "Should the lamp of religion be obscured, chaos and confusion will ensue, and the lights of fairness, of justice, of tranquillity and peace cease to shine." In an enumeration of such consequences the Bahá'í writings point out that the "perversion of human nature, the degradation of human conduct, the corruption and dissolution of human institutions, reveal themselves, under such circumstances, in their worst and most revolting aspects. Human character is debased, confidence is shaken, the nerves of discipline are relaxed, the voice of human conscience is stilled, the sense of decency and shame is obscured, conceptions of duty, of solidarity, of reciprocity and loyalty are distorted, and the very feeling of peacefulness, of joy and of hope is gradually extinguished."

If, therefore, humanity has come to a point of paralyzing conflict it must look to itself, to its own negligence, to the siren voices to which it has listened, for the source of the misunderstandings and confusion perpetrated in the name of religion. Those who have held blindly and selfishly to their particular orthodoxies, who have imposed on their votaries erroneous and conflicting interpretations of the pronouncements of the Prophets of God, bear heavy responsibility for this confusion—a confusion compounded by the artificial barriers erected between faith and reason, science and religion. For from a fair-minded examination of the actual utterances of the Founders of the great religions, and of the social milieus in which they were obliged to carry out their missions, there is nothing to support the contentions and prejudices deranging the religious communities of mankind and therefore all human affairs.

The teaching that we should treat others as we ourselves would wish to be treated, an ethic variously repeated in all the great religions, lends force to this latter observation in two particular respects: it sums up the moral attitude, the peace-inducing aspect, extending through these religions irrespective of their place or time of origin; it also signifies an aspect of unity which is their essential virtue, a virtue mankind in its disjointed view of history has failed to appreciate.

Had humanity seen the educators of its collective childhood in their true character, as agents of one civilizing process, it would no doubt have reaped incalculably greater benefits from the cumulative effects of their successive missions. This, alas, it failed to do.

The resurgence of fanatical religious fervor occurring in many lands cannot be regarded as more than a dying convulsion. The very nature of the violent and disruptive phenomena associated with it testifies to the spiritual bankruptcy it represents. Indeed, one of the strangest and saddest features of the current outbreak of religious fanaticism is the extent to which, in each case, it is undermining not only the spiritual values which are conducive to the unity of mankind but also those unique moral victories won by the particular religion it purports to serve.

However vital a force religion has been in the history of mankind, and however dramatic the current resurgence of militant religious fanaticism, religion and religious institutions have, for many decades, been viewed by increasing numbers of people as irrelevant to the major concerns of the modern world. In its place they have turned either to the hedonistic pursuit of material satisfactions or to the following of man-made ideologies designed to rescue society from the evident evils under which it groans. All too many of these ideologies, alas, instead of embracing the concept of the oneness of mankind and promoting the increase of concord among different peoples, have tended to deify the state, to subordinate the rest of mankind to one nation, race or class, to attempt to suppress all discussion and interchange of ideas, or to callously abandon starving millions to the operations of a market system that all too clearly is aggravating the plight of the majority of mankind, while enabling small sections to live in a condition of affluence scarcely dreamed of by our forebears.

How tragic is the record of the substitute faiths that the worldly wise of our age have created. In the massive disillusionment of entire populations who have been taught to worship at their altars can be read history's irreversible verdict on their value. The fruits these doctrines have produced after decades of an increasingly unrestrained exercise of power by those who owe their ascendancy in human affairs to them, are the social and economic ills that blight every region of our world in the closing years of the twentieth century. Underlying all these outward afflictions is the spiritual damage reflected in the apathy that has gripped the mass of the peoples of all nations and by the extinction of hope in the hearts of deprived and anguished millions.

The time has come when those who preach the dogmas of materialism, whether of the east or the west, whether of capitalism or socialism, must give account of the moral stewardship they have presumed to exercise. Where is the "new world" promised by these ideologies? Where is the international peace to whose ideals they proclaim their devotion? Where are the breakthroughs into new realms of cultural achievement produced by the aggrandizement of this race, of that nation or of a particular class? Why is the vast majority of the world's peoples sinking ever deeper into hunger and wretchedness when wealth on a scale undreamed of by the Pharaohs, the Caesars, or even the imperialist powers of the nineteenth century is at the disposal of the present arbiters of human affairs?

Most particularly, it is in the glorification of material pursuits, at once the progenitor and common feature of all such ideologies, that we find the roots which nourish the falsehood that human beings are incorrigibly selfish and aggressive. It is here that the ground must be cleared for the building of a new world fit for our descendants.

That materialistic ideals have, in the light of experience, failed to satisfy the needs of mankind calls for an honest acknowledgment that a fresh effort must now be made to find the solutions to the agonizing problems of the planet. The intolerable conditions pervading society bespeak a common failure of all, a circumstance which tends to incite rather than relieve the entrenchment on every side. Clearly, a common remedial effort is urgently required. It is primarily a matter of attitude. Will humanity continue in its waywardness, holding to outworn concepts and unworkable assumptions? Or will its leaders, regardless of ideology, step forth and, with a resolute will, consult together in a united search for appropriate solutions?

Those who care for the future of the human race may well ponder this advice. "If long-cherished ideals and time-honored institutions, if certain social assumptions and religious formulae have ceased to promote the welfare of the generality of mankind, if they no longer minister to the needs of a continually evolving humanity, let them be swept away and relegated to the limbo of obsolescent and forgotten doctrines. Why should these, in a world subject to the immutable law of change and decay, be exempt from the deterioration that must needs overtake every human institution? For legal standards, political and economic theories are solely designed to safeguard the interests of humanity as a whole, and not humanity to be crucified for the preservation of the integrity of any particular law or doctrine."

II

Banning nuclear weapons, prohibiting the use of poison gases, or outlawing germ warfare will not remove the root causes of war. However important such practical measures obviously are as elements of the peace process, they are in themselves too superficial to exert enduring influence. Peoples are ingenious enough to invent yet other forms of warfare, and to use food, raw materials, finance, industrial power, ideology, and terrorism to subvert one another in an endless quest for supremacy and dominion. Nor can the present massive dislocation in the affairs of humanity be resolved through the settlement of specific conflicts or disagreements among nations. A genuine universal framework must be adopted.

Certainly, there is no lack of recognition by national leaders of the worldwide character of the problem, which is self-evident in the mounting issues that confront them daily. And there are the accumulating studies and solutions proposed by many concerned and enlightened groups as well as by agencies of the United Nations, to remove any possibility of ignorance as to the challenging requirements to be met. There is, however, a paralysis of will; and it is this that must be carefully examined and resolutely dealt with. This paralysis is rooted, as we have stated, in a deep-seated conviction of the inevitable quarrelsomeness of mankind, which has led to the reluctance to entertain the possibility of subordinating national self-interest to the requirements of world order, and in an unwillingness to face courageously the far-reaching implications of establishing a united world authority. It is also traceable to the incapacity of largely ignorant and subjugated masses to articulate their desire for a new order in which they can live in peace, harmony and prosperity with all humanity.

The tentative steps towards world order, especially since World War II, give hopeful signs. The increasing tendency of groups of nations to formalize relationships which enable them to cooperate in matters of mutual interest suggests that eventually all nations could overcome this paralysis. The Association of South East Asian Nations, the Caribbean Community and Common Market, the Central American Common Market, the Council for Mutual Economic Assistance, the European Communities, the League of Arab States, the Organization of African Unity, the Organization of American States, the South Pacific Forum—all the joint endeavors represented by such organizations prepare the path to world order.

The increasing attention being focused on some of the most deep-rooted problems of the planet is yet another hopeful sign. Despite the obvious shortcomings of the United Nations, the more than two score declarations and conventions adopted by that organization, even where governments have not been enthusiastic in their commitment, have given ordinary people a sense of a new lease on life. The Universal Declaration of Human Rights, the Convention on the Prevention and Punishment of the Crime of Genocide, and the similar measures concerned with eliminating all forms of discrimination based on race, sex or religious belief; upholding the rights of the child; protecting all persons against being subjected to torture; eradicating hunger and malnutrition; using scientific and technological progress in the interest of peace and the benefit of mankind—all such measures, if courageously enforced and expanded, will advance the day when the specter of war will have lost its power to dominate international relations. There is no need to stress the significance of the issues addressed by these declarations and conventions. However, a few such issues, because of their immediate relevance to establishing world peace, deserve additional comment.

Racism, one of the most baneful and persistent evils, is a major barrier to peace. Its practice perpetrates too outrageous a violation of the dignity of human beings to be countenanced under any pretext. Racism retards the unfoldment of the boundless potentialities of its victims, corrupts its perpetrators, and blights human progress. Recognition of the oneness of mankind, implemented by appropriate legal measures, must be universally upheld if this problem is to be overcome.

The inordinate disparity between rich and poor, a source of acute suffering, keeps the world in a state of instability, virtually on the brink of war. Few societies have dealt effectively with this situation. The solution calls for the combined application of spiritual, moral and practical approaches. A fresh look at the problem is required, entailing consultation with experts from a wide spectrum of disciplines, devoid of economic and ideological polemics, and involving the people directly affected in the decisions that must urgently be made. It is an issue that is bound up not only with the necessity for eliminating extremes of wealth and poverty but also with those spiritual verities the understanding of which can produce a new universal attitude. Fostering such an attitude is itself a major part of the solution.

Unbridled nationalism, as distinguished from a sane and legitimate patriotism, must give way to a wider loyalty, to the love of humanity as a whole. Bahá'u'lláh's statement is: "The earth is but one country, and mankind its citizens." The concept of world citizenship is a direct result of the contraction of the world into a single neighborhood through scientific advances and of the indisputable interdependence of nations. Love of all the world's peoples does not exclude love of one's country. The advantage of the part in a world society is best served by promoting the advantage of the whole. Current international activities in various fields which nurture mutual affection and a sense of solidarity among peoples need greatly to be increased.

Religious strife, throughout history, has been the cause of innumerable wars and conflicts, a major blight to progress, and is increasingly abhorrent to the people of all faiths and no faith. Followers of all religions must be willing to face the basic questions which this strife raises, and to arrive at clear answers. How are the differences between them to be resolved, both in theory and in practice? The challenge facing the religious leaders of mankind is to contemplate, with hearts filled with the spirit of compassion and a desire for truth, the plight of humanity, and to ask themselves whether they cannot, in humility before their Almighty Creator, submerge their theological differences in a great spirit of mutual forbearance that will enable them to work together for the advancement of human understanding and peace.

The emancipation of women, the achievement of full equality between the sexes, is one of the most important, though less acknowledged prerequisites of peace. The denial of such equality perpetrates an injustice against one half of the world's population and promotes in men harmful attitudes and habits that are carried from the family to the workplace, to political life, and ultimately to international relations. There are no grounds, moral, practical, or biological, upon which such denial can be justified. Only as women are welcomed into full partnership in all fields of human endeavor will the moral and psychological climate be created in which international peace can emerge.

The cause of universal education, which has already enlisted in its service an army of dedicated people from every faith and nation, deserves the utmost support that the governments of the world can lend it. For ignorance is indisputably the principal reason for the decline and fall of peoples and the perpetuation of prejudice. No nation can achieve success unless education is accorded all its citizens. Lack of resources limits the ability of many nations to fulfill this necessity, imposing a certain ordering of priorities. The decision-making agencies involved would do well to consider giving first priority to the education of women and girls, since it is through educated mothers that the benefits of knowledge can be most effectively and rapidly diffused throughout society. In keeping with the requirements of the times, consideration should also be given to teaching the concept of world citizenship as part of the standard education of every child.

A fundamental lack of communication between peoples seriously undermines efforts towards world peace. Adopting an international auxiliary language would go far to resolving this problem and necessitates the most urgent attention.

Two points bear emphasizing in all these issues. One is that the abolition of war is not simply a matter of signing treaties and protocols; it is a complex task requiring a new level of commitment to resolving issues not customarily associated with the pursuit of peace. Based on political agreements alone, the idea of collective security is a chimera. The other point is that the primary challenge in dealing with issues of peace is to raise the context to the level of principle, as distinct from pure pragmatism. For, in essence, peace stems from an inner state supported by a spiritual or moral attitude, and it is chiefly in evoking this attitude that the possibility of enduring solutions can be found.

There are spiritual principles, or what some call human values, by which solutions can be found for every social problem. Any well-intentioned group can in a general sense devise practical solutions to its problems, but good intentions and practical knowledge are usually not enough. The essential merit of spiritual principle is that it not only presents a perspective which harmonizes with that which is immanent in human nature, it also induces an attitude, a dynamic, a will, an aspiration, which facilitate the discovery and implementation of practical measures. Leaders of governments and all in authority would be well served in their efforts to solve problems if they would first seek to identify the principles involved and then be guided by them.

III

The primary question to be resolved is how the present world, with its entrenched pattern of conflict, can change to a world in which harmony and cooperation will prevail.

World order can be founded only on an unshakable consciousness of the oneness of mankind, a spiritual truth which all the human sciences confirm. Anthropology, physiology, psychology, recognize only one human species, albeit infinitely varied in the secondary aspects of life. Recognition of this truth requires abandonment of prejudice—prejudice of every kind—race, class, color, creed, nation, sex, degree of material civilization, everything which enables people to consider themselves superior to others.

Acceptance of the oneness of mankind is the first fundamental prerequisite for reorganization and administration of the world as one country, the home of humankind. Universal acceptance of this spiritual principle is essential to any successful attempt to establish world peace. It should therefore be universally proclaimed, taught in schools, and constantly asserted in every nation as preparation for the organic change in the structure of society which it implies.

In the Bahá'í view, recognition of the oneness of mankind "calls for no less than the reconstruction and the demilitarization of the whole civilized world—a world organically unified in all the essential aspects of its life, its political machinery, its spiritual aspiration, its trade and finance, its script and language, and yet infinite in the diversity of the national characteristics of its federated units."

Elaborating the implications of this pivotal principle, Shoghi Effendi, the Guardian of the Bahá'í Faith, commented in 1931 that: "Far from aiming at the subversion of the existing foundations of society, it seeks to broaden its basis, to remold its institutions in a manner consonant with the needs of an ever-changing world. It can conflict with no legitimate allegiances, nor can it undermine essential loyalties. Its purpose is neither to stifle the flame of a sane and intelligent patriotism in men's hearts, nor to abolish the system of national autonomy so essential if the evils of excessive centralization are to be avoided. It does not ignore, nor does it attempt to suppress, the diversity of ethnical origins, of climate, of history, of language and tradition, of thought and habit, that differentiate the peoples and nations of the world. It calls for a wider loyalty, for a larger aspiration than any that has animated the human race. It insists upon the subordination of national impulses and interests to the imperative claims of a unified world. It repudiates excessive centralization on one hand, and disclaims all attempts at uniformity on the other. Its watchword is unity in diversity. . . ."

The achievement of such ends requires several stages in the adjustment of national political attitudes, which now verge on anarchy in the absence of clearly defined laws or universally accepted and enforceable principles regulating the relationships between nations. The League of Nations, the United Nations, and the many organizations and agreements produced by them have unquestionably been helpful in attenuating some of the negative effects of international conflicts, but they have shown themselves incapable of preventing war. Indeed, there have been scores of wars since the end of the Second World War; many are yet raging.

The predominant aspects of this problem had already emerged in the nineteenth century when Bahá'u'lláh first advanced his proposals for the establishment of world peace. The principle of collective security was propounded by him in statements addressed to the rulers of the world. Shoghi Effendi commented on his meaning: "What else could these weighty words signify," he wrote, "if they did not point to the inevitable curtailment of unfettered national sovereignty as an indispensable preliminary to the formation of the future Commonwealth of all the nations of the world? Some form of a world superstate must needs be evolved, in whose favor all the nations of the world will have willingly ceded every claim to make war, certain rights to impose taxation and all rights to maintain armaments, except for purposes of maintaining internal order within their respective dominions. Such a state will have to include within its orbit an International Executive adequate to enforce supreme and unchallengeable authority on every recalcitrant member of the commonwealth; a World Parliament whose members shall be elected by the people in their respective countries and whose election shall be confirmed by their respective governments; and a Supreme Tribunal whose judgment will have a binding effect even in such cases where the parties concerned did not voluntarily agree to submit their case to its consideration.

"A world community in which all economic barriers will have been permanently demolished and the interdependence of capital and labor definitely recognized; in which the clamor of religious fanaticism and strife will have been forever stilled; in which the flame of racial animosity will have been finally extinguished; in which a single code of international law—the product of the considered judgment of the world's federated representatives—shall have as its sanction the instant and coercive intervention of the combined forces of the federated units; and finally a world community in which the fury of a capricious and militant nationalism will have been transmuted into an abiding consciousness of world citizenship—such indeed, appears, in its broadest outline, the Order anticipated by Bahá'u'lláh, an Order that shall come to be regarded as the fairest fruit of a slowly maturing age."

The implementation of these far-reaching measures was indicated by Bahá'u'lláh: "The time must come when the imperative necessity for the holding of a vast, an all-embracing assemblage of men will be universally realized. The rulers and kings of the earth must needs attend it, and, participating in its deliberations, must consider such ways and means as will lay the foundations of the world's Great Peace amongst men."

The courage, the resolution, the pure motive, the selfless love of one people for another—all the spiritual and moral qualities required for effecting this momentous step towards peace are focused on the will to act. And it is towards arousing the necessary volition that earnest consideration must be given to the reality of man, namely, his thought. To understand the relevance of this potent reality is also to appreciate the social necessity of actualizing its unique value through candid, dispassionate and cordial consultation, and of acting upon the results of this process. Bahá'u'lláh insistently drew attention to the virtues and indispensability of consultation for ordering human affairs. He said: "Consultation bestows greater awareness and transmutes conjecture into certitude. It is a shining light which, in a dark world, leads the way and guides. For everything there is and will continue to be a station of perfection and maturity. The maturity of the gift of understanding is made manifest through consultation." The very attempt to achieve peace through the consultative action he proposed can release such a salutary spirit among the peoples of the earth that no power could resist the final, triumphal outcome.

Concerning the proceedings for this world gathering, 'Abdu'l-Bahá, the son of Bahá'u'lláh, and authorized interpreter of his teachings, offered these insights: "They must make the Cause of Peace the object of general consultation, and seek by every means in their power to establish a Union of the nations of the world. They must conclude a binding treaty and establish a covenant, the provisions of which shall be sound, inviolable and definite. They must proclaim it to all the world and obtain for it the sanction of all the human race. This supreme and noble undertaking—the real source of the peace and well-being of all the world—should be regarded as sacred by all that dwell on earth. All the forces of humanity must be mobilized to ensure the stability and permanence of this Most Great Covenant. In this all-embracing Pact the limits and frontiers of each and every nation should be clearly fixed, the principles underlying the relations of governments towards one another definitely laid down, and all international agreements and obligations ascertained. In like manner, the size of the armaments of every government should be strictly limited, for if the preparations for war and the military forces of any nation should be allowed to increase, they will arouse the suspicion of others. The fundamental principle underlying this solemn Pact should be so fixed that if any government later violate any one of its provisions, all the governments on earth should arise to reduce it to utter submission, nay the human race as a whole should resolve, with every power at its disposal, to destroy that government. Should this greatest of all remedies be applied to the sick body of the world, it will assuredly recover from its ills and will remain eternally safe and secure."

The holding of this mighty convocation is long overdue.

With all the ardor of our hearts, we appeal to the leaders of all nations to seize this opportune moment and take irreversible steps to convoke this world meeting. All the forces of history impel the human race towards this act which will mark for all time the dawn of its long-awaited maturity.

Will not the United Nations, with the full support of its membership, rise to the high purposes of such a crowning event?

Let men and women, youth and children everywhere recognize the eternal merit of this imperative action for all peoples and lift up their voices in willing assent. Indeed, let it be this generation that inaugurates this glorious stage in the evolution of social life on the planet.

IV

The source of the optimism we feel is a vision transcending the cessation of war and the creation of agencies of international cooperation. Permanent peace among nations is an essential stage, but not, Bahá'u'lláh asserts, the ultimate goal of the social development of humanity. Beyond the initial armistice forced upon the world by the fear of nuclear holocaust, beyond the political peace reluctantly entered into by suspicious rival nations, beyond pragmatic arrangements for security and coexistence, beyond even the many experiments in cooperation which these steps will make possible lies the crowning goal: the unification of all the peoples of the world in one universal family.

Disunity is a danger that the nations and peoples of the earth can no longer endure; the consequences are too terrible to contemplate, too obvious to require any demonstration. "The well-being of mankind," Bahá'u'lláh wrote more than a century ago, "its peace and security, are unattainable unless and until its unity is firmly established." In observing that "mankind is groaning, is dying to be led to unity, and to terminate its agelong martyrdom," Shoghi Effendi further commented that: "Unification of the whole of mankind is the hallmark of the stage which human society is now approaching. Unity of family, of tribe, of city-state, and nation have been successively attempted and fully established. World unity is the goal towards which a harassed humanity is striving. Nation-building has come to an end. The anarchy inherent in state sovereignty is moving towards a climax. A world, growing to maturity, must abandon this fetish, recognize the oneness and wholeness of human relationships, and establish once for all the machinery that can best incarnate this fundamental principle of its life."

All contemporary forces of change validate this view. The proofs can be discerned in the many examples already cited of the favorable signs towards world peace in current international movements and developments. The army of men and women, drawn from virtually every culture, race and nation on earth, who serve the multifarious agencies of the United Nations, represent a planetary "civil service" whose impressive accomplishments are indicative of the degree of cooperation that can be attained even under discouraging conditions. An urge towards unity, like a spiritual springtime, struggles to express itself through countless international congresses that bring together people from a vast array of disciplines. It motivates appeals for international projects involving children and youth. Indeed, it is the real source of the remarkable movement towards ecumenism by which members of historically antagonistic religions and sects seem irresistibly drawn towards one another. Together with the opposing tendency to warfare and self-aggrandizement against which it ceaselessly struggles, the drive towards world unity is one of the dominant, pervasive features of life on the planet during the closing years of the twentieth century.

The experience of the Bahá'í community may be seen as an example of this enlarging unity. It is a community of some three to four million people drawn from many nations, cultures, classes and creeds, engaged in a wide range of activities serving the spiritual, social and economic needs of the peoples of many lands. It is a single social organism, representative of the diversity of the human family, conducting its affairs through a system of commonly accepted consultative principles, and cherishing equally all the great outpourings of divine guidance in human history. Its existence is yet another convincing proof of the practicality of its Founder's vision of a united world, another evidence that humanity can live as one global society, equal to whatever challenges its coming of age may entail. If the Bahá'í experience can contribute in whatever measure to reinforcing hope in the unity of the human race, we are happy to offer it as a model for study.

In contemplating the supreme importance of the task now challenging the entire world, we bow our heads in humility before the awesome majesty of the divine Creator, Who out of His infinite love has created all humanity from the same stock; exalted the gemlike reality of man; honored it with intellect and wisdom, nobility and immortality; and conferred upon man the "unique distinction and capacity to know Him and to love Him," a capacity that "must needs be regarded as the generating impulse and the primary purpose underlying the whole of creation."

We hold firmly the conviction that all human beings have been created "to carry forward an ever-advancing civilization"; that "to act like the beasts of the field is unworthy of man"; that the virtues that befit human dignity are trustworthiness, forbearance, mercy, compassion and loving kindness towards all peoples. We reaffirm the belief that the "potentialities inherent in the station of man, the full measure of his destiny on earth, the innate excellence of his reality, must all be manifested in this promised Day of God." These are the motivations for our unshakable faith that unity and peace are the attainable goal towards which humanity is striving.

At this writing, the expectant voices of Bahá'ís can be heard despite the persecution they still endure in the land in which their Faith was born. By their example of steadfast hope, they bear witness to the belief that the imminent realization of this age-old dream of peace is now, by virtue of the transforming effects of Bahá'u'lláh's revelation, invested with the force of divine authority. Thus we convey to you not only a vision in words: we summon the power of deeds of faith and sacrifice; we convey the anxious plea of our coreligionists everywhere for peace and unity. We join with all who are the victims of aggression, all who yearn for an end to conflict and contention, all whose devotion to principles of peace and world order promotes the ennobling purposes for which humanity was called into being by an all-loving Creator.

In the earnestness of our desire to impart to you the fervor of our hope and the depth of our confidence, we cite the emphatic promise of Bahá'u'lláh: "These fruitless strifes, these ruinous wars shall pass away, and the 'Most Great Peace' shall come."

—*The Universal House of Justice*

II

PRAYERS AND WRITINGS

Aid and Assistance

Bahá'u'lláh—may my life, my soul, my spirit be offered up as a sacrifice unto His lowly servants—hath, during His last days on earth, given the most emphatic promise that, through the outpourings of the grace of God and the aid and assistance vouchsafed from His Kingdom on high, souls will arise and holy beings appear who, as stars, would adorn the firmament of divine guidance; illumine the dayspring of loving-kindness and bounty; manifest the signs of the unity of God; shine with the light of sanctity and purity; receive their full measure of divine inspiration; raise high the sacred torch of faith; stand firm as the rock and immoveable as the mountain; and grow to become luminaries in the heavens of His Revelation, mighty channels of His grace, means for the bestowal of God's bountiful care, heralds calling forth the name of the One true God, and establishers of the world's supreme foundation.

—*'Abdu'l-Bahá,* SELECTIONS FROM THE WRITINGS OF 'ABDU'L-BAHÁ

1

Thou beholdest, O my God, Thy servant who dwelleth in this prison-house, wholly detached from any one but Thee, his eyes turned in the direction of the Day-Spring of Thy mercy, his heart longing for the wondrous manifestations of Thy grace. Thou, O my Lord, hast reckoned up the ills that have afflicted him in Thy path. Thou seest him compassed about with such of Thy creatures as have transgressed and rebelled against Thee, who have come in between him and Thy loved ones, who have fixed his abode in this land and wronged Thee, and who have hindered Thy servants from turning towards Thee.

For all these things I offer thanksgiving unto Thee, O my Lord! I implore Thee to assist me and them that love me to magnify Thy Word, and to endow us with such strength that the ills of this world and its tribulations will be powerless to hinder us from remembering Thee and from extolling Thy virtues. Powerful art Thou to do all things; resplendent art Thou above all things.

Every conqueror is but a serf whom Thy hand hath subjected, and the richest of the rich is as destitute before the immensity of Thy wealth. The noblest of nobles is humbled when faced with the manifestations of Thy glory, and the mightiest of potentates is a mere abject one when confronted with the compelling evidences of Thine authority.

Tear asunder, O my God, the veil of vain imaginings that hath obscured the vision of Thy people, that all may haste towards Thee, may tread the path of Thy pleasure, and walk in the ways of Thy Faith. We are, O my God, Thy servants and Thy bondsmen. Thou art sufficient unto us so that we can dispense with the world and all that is therein. We are wholly satisfied with all that hath befallen us in Thy path, and exclaim: "Praised be Thou, in Whose hand are the realms of revelation and of creation, and all the kingdoms of earth and heaven!"

—*Bahá'u'lláh*

2

O Thou kind Lord! We are servants of Thy Threshold, taking shelter at Thy holy Door. We seek no refuge save only this strong pillar, turn nowhere for a haven but unto Thy safekeeping. Protect us, bless us, support us, make us such that we shall love but Thy good pleasure, utter only Thy praise, follow only the pathway of truth, that we may become rich enough to dispense with all save Thee, and receive our gifts from the sea of Thy beneficence, that we may ever strive to exalt Thy Cause and to spread Thy sweet savors far and wide, that we may become oblivious of self and occupied only with Thee, and disown all else and be caught up in Thee. O Thou Provider, O Thou Forgiver! Grant us Thy grace and loving-kindness, Thy gifts and Thy bestowals, and sustain us, that we may attain our goal. Thou art the Powerful, the Able, the Knower, the Seer; and, verily, Thou art the Generous, and, verily, Thou art the All-Merciful, and, verily, Thou art the Ever-Forgiving, He to Whom repentance is due, He Who forgiveth even the most grievous of sins.

—*'Abdu'l-Bahá*

3

Lord! Pitiful are we, grant us Thy favor; poor, bestow upon us a share from the ocean of Thy wealth; needy, do Thou satisfy us; abased, give us Thy glory. The fowls of the air and the beasts of the field receive their meat each day from Thee, and all beings partake of Thy care and loving-kindness.

Deprive not this feeble one of Thy wondrous grace and vouchsafe by Thy might unto this helpless soul Thy bounty.

Give us our daily bread, and grant Thine increase in the necessities of life, that we may be dependent on none other but Thee, may commune wholly with Thee, may walk in Thy ways and declare Thy mysteries. Thou art the Almighty and the Loving and the Provider of all mankind.

—*'Abdu'l-Bahá*

4

Remove not, O Lord, the festal board that hath been spread in Thy Name, and extinguish not the burning flame that hath been kindled by Thine unquenchable fire. Withhold not from flowing that living water of Thine that murmureth with the melody of Thy glory and Thy remembrance, and deprive not Thy servants from the fragrance of Thy sweet savors breathing forth the perfume of Thy love. Lord! Turn the distressing cares of Thy holy ones into ease, their hardship into comfort, their abasement into glory, their sorrow into blissful joy, O Thou that holdest in Thy grasp the reins of all mankind! Thou art, verily, the One, the Single, the Mighty, the All-Knowing, the All-Wise.

—*'Abdu'l-Bahá*

America

America has developed powers and capacities greater and more wonderful than other nations. While it is true that its people have attained a marvelous material civilization, I hope that spiritual forces may animate this great body and a corresponding spiritual civilization be established. May the inhabitants of this country become like angels of heaven with faces turned continually toward God. May all of them become the servants of the Omnipotent One. May they rise from present material attainments to such a height that heavenly illumination may stream from this center to all the peoples of the world.

—*'Abdu'l-Bahá,* The Promulgation of Universal Peace

1

O Thou kind Lord! This gathering is turning to Thee. These hearts are radiant with Thy love. These minds and spirits are exhilarated by the message of Thy glad-tidings. O God! Let this American democracy become glorious in spiritual degrees even as it has aspired to material degrees, and render this just government victorious. Confirm this revered nation to upraise the standard of the oneness of humanity, to promulgate the Most Great Peace, to become thereby most glorious and praiseworthy among all the nations of the world. O God! This American nation is worthy of Thy favors and is deserving of Thy mercy. Make it precious and near to Thee through Thy bounty and bestowal.

—*'Abdu'l-Bahá*

Children

While the children are yet in their infancy feed them from the breast of heavenly grace, foster them in the cradle of all excellence, rear them in the embrace of bounty. Give them the advantage of every useful kind of knowledge. Let them share in every new and rare and wondrous craft and art. Bring them up to work and strive, and accustom them to hardship. Teach them to dedicate their lives to matters of great import, and inspire them to undertake studies that will benefit mankind.

—*'Abdu'l-Bahá,* SELECTIONS FROM THE WRITINGS OF 'ABDU'L-BAHÁ

1

Praised be Thou, O Lord my God! Graciously grant that this infant be fed from the breast of Thy tender mercy and loving providence and be nourished with the fruit of Thy celestial trees. Suffer him not to be committed to the care of anyone save Thee, inasmuch as Thou, Thyself, through the potency of Thy sovereign will and power, didst create and call him into being. There is none other God but Thee, the Almighty, the All-Knowing.

Lauded art Thou, O my Best Beloved, waft over him the sweet savors of Thy transcendent bounty and the fragrances of Thy holy bestowals. Enable him then to seek shelter beneath the shadow of Thy most exalted Name, O Thou Who holdest in Thy grasp the kingdom of names and attributes. Verily, Thou art potent to do what Thou willest, and Thou art indeed the Mighty, the Exalted, the Ever-Forgiving, the Gracious, the Generous, the Merciful.

—*Bahá'u'lláh*

2

O God! Educate these children. These children are the plants of Thine orchard, the flowers of Thy meadow, the roses of Thy garden. Let Thy rain fall upon them; let the Sun of Reality shine upon them with Thy love. Let Thy breeze refresh them in order that they may be trained, grow and develop, and appear in the utmost beauty. Thou art the Giver. Thou art the Compassionate.

—*'Abdu'l-Bahá*

3

O Thou kind Lord! These lovely children are the handiwork of the fingers of Thy might and the wondrous signs of Thy greatness. O God! Protect these children, graciously assist them to be educated and enable them to render service to the world of humanity. O God! These children are pearls, cause them to be nurtured within the shell of Thy loving-kindness. Thou art the Bountiful, the All-Loving.

—*'Abdu'l-Bahá*

4

O God! Rear this little babe in the bosom of Thy love, and give it milk from the breast of Thy Providence. Cultivate this fresh plant in the rose garden of Thy love and aid it to grow through the showers of Thy bounty. Make it a child of the kingdom, and lead it to Thy heavenly realm. Thou art powerful and kind, and Thou art the Bestower, the Generous, the Lord of surpassing bounty.

—*'Abdu'l-Bahá*

5

O Lord! Make these children excellent plants. Let them grow and develop in the Garden of Thy Covenant, and bestow freshness and beauty through the outpourings of the clouds of the Abhá Kingdom.

O Thou kind Lord! I am a little child, exalt me by admitting me to the kingdom. I am earthly, make me heavenly; I am of the world below, let me belong to the realm above; gloomy, suffer me to become radiant; material, make me spiritual, and grant that I may manifest Thine infinite bounties.

Thou art the Powerful, the All-Loving.

—*'Abdu'l-Bahá*

6

O Peerless Lord! Be Thou a shelter for this poor child and a kind and forgiving Master unto this erring and unhappy soul. O Lord! Though we are but worthless plants, yet we belong to Thy garden of roses. Though saplings without leaves and blossoms, yet we are a part of Thine orchard. Nurture this plant then through the outpourings of the clouds of Thy tender mercy and quicken and refresh this sapling through the reviving breath of Thy spiritual springtime. Suffer him to become heedful, discerning and noble, and grant that he may attain eternal life and abide in Thy Kingdom for evermore.

—*'Abdu'l-Bahá*

For the Departed

O Son of the Supreme! I have made death a messenger of joy to thee. Wherefore dost thou grieve? I made the light to shed on thee its splendor. Why dost thou veil thyself therefrom?

—*Bahá'u'lláh,* The Hidden Words

1

Glory be to Thee, O Lord my God! Abase not him whom Thou hast exalted through the power of Thine everlasting sovereignty, and remove not far from Thee him whom Thou hast caused to enter the tabernacle of Thine eternity. Wilt Thou cast away, O my God, him whom thou hast overshadowed with Thy Lordship, and wilt Thou turn away from Thee, O my Desire, him to whom Thou hast been a refuge? Canst Thou degrade him whom Thou hast uplifted, or forget him whom Thou didst enable to remember Thee?

Glorified, immensely glorified art Thou! Thou art He Who from everlasting hath been the King of the entire creation and its Prime Mover, and Thou wilt to everlasting remain the Lord of all created things and their Ordainer. Glorified art Thou, O my God! If Thou ceasest to be merciful unto Thy servants, who, then, will show mercy unto them; and if Thou refusest to succor thy loved ones, who is there that can succor them?

Glorified, immeasurably glorified art Thou! Thou art adored in Thy truth, and Thee do we all, verily, worship; and Thou art manifest in Thy justice, and to Thee do we all, verily, bear witness.

Thou art, in truth, beloved in Thy grace. No God is there but Thee, the Help in Peril, the Self-Subsisting.

—*Bahá'u'lláh*

2

O my God! O Thou forgiver of sins, bestower of gifts, dispeller of afflictions! Verily, I beseech Thee to forgive the sins of such as have abandoned the physical garment and have ascended to the spiritual world. O my Lord! Purify them from trespasses, dispel their sorrows, and change their darkness into light. Cause them to enter the garden of happiness, cleanse them with the most pure water, and grant them to behold Thy splendors on the loftiest mount.

—*'Abdu'l-Bahá*

3

O Thou forgiving Lord! Although some souls have spent the days of their lives in ignorance, and became estranged and contumacious, yet, with one wave from the ocean of Thy forgiveness, all those encompassed by sin will be set free. Whomsoever Thou willest Thou makest a confidant, and whosoever is not the object of Thy choice is accounted a transgressor. Shouldst Thou deal with us with Thy justice, we are all naught but sinners and deserving to be shut out from Thee, but shouldst Thou uphold mercy, every sinner would be made pure and every stranger a friend. Bestow, then, Thy forgiveness and pardon, and grant Thy mercy unto all. Thou art the Forgiver, the Lightgiver and the Omnipotent.

—*'Abdu'l-Bahá*

4

O my God! O my God! Verily, Thy servant, humble before the majesty of Thy divine supremacy, lowly at the door of Thy oneness, hath believed in Thee and in Thy verses, hath testified to Thy word, hath been enkindled with the fire of Thy love, hath been immersed in the depths of the ocean of Thy knowledge, hath been attracted by Thy breezes, hath relied upon Thee, hath offered his supplications to Thee, and hath been assured of Thy pardon and forgiveness. He hath abandoned this mortal life and hath flown to the kingdom of immortality, yearning for the favor of meeting Thee.

O Lord, glorify his station, shelter him under the pavilion of Thy supreme mercy, cause him to enter Thy glorious paradise, and perpetuate his existence in Thine exalted rose garden, that he may plunge into the sea of light in the world of mysteries.

Verily, Thou art the Generous, the Powerful, the Forgiver and the Bestower.

—*'Abdu'l-Bahá*

Evening

Among the proofs of the existence of a divine power is this: that things are often known by their opposites. Were it not for darkness, light could not be sensed. Were it not for death, life could not be known. If ignorance did not exist, knowledge would not be a reality. It is necessary that each should exist in order that the other should have reality. Night and day must be in order that each may be distinguished. Night itself is an indication and evidence of day which follows, and day itself indicates the coming night. Unless night were a reality, there could not be day. Were it not for death, there could be no life. Things are known by their opposites.

—*'Abdu'l-Bahá,* THE PROMULGATION OF UNIVERSAL PEACE

1

O my God, my Master, the Goal of my desire! This, Thy servant, seeketh to sleep in the shelter of Thy mercy, and to repose beneath the canopy of Thy grace, imploring Thy care and Thy protection. I beg of Thee, O my Lord, by Thine eye that sleepeth not, to guard mine eyes from beholding aught beside Thee. Strengthen, then, their vision that they may discern Thy signs, and behold the Horizon of Thy Revelation. Thou art He before the revelations of Whose omnipotence the quintessence of power hath trembled. No God is there but Thee, the Almighty, the All-Subduing, the Unconditioned.

—Bahá'u'lláh

2

How can I choose to sleep, O God, my God, when the eyes of them that long for Thee are wakeful because of their separation from Thee; and how can I lie down to rest whilst the souls of Thy lovers are sore vexed in their remoteness from Thy presence? I have committed, O my Lord, my spirit and my entire being into the right hand of Thy might and Thy protection, and I lay my head on my pillow through Thy power, and lift it up according to Thy will and Thy good pleasure. Thou art, in truth, the Preserver, the Keeper, the Almighty, the Most Powerful. By Thy might! I ask not, whether sleeping or waking, but that which Thou dost desire. I am Thy servant and in Thy hands. Do Thou graciously aid me to do what will shed forth the fragrance of Thy good pleasure. This, truly, is my hope and the hope of them that enjoy near access to Thee. Praised be Thou, O Lord of the worlds!

—*Bahá'u'lláh*

3

O seeker of Truth! If thou desirest that God may open thine eye, thou must supplicate unto God, pray to and commune with Him at midnight, saying:

O Lord, I have turned my face unto Thy kingdom of oneness and am immersed in the sea of Thy mercy. O Lord, enlighten my sight by beholding Thy lights in this dark night, and make me happy by the wine of Thy love in this wonderful age. O Lord, make me hear Thy call, and open before my face the doors of Thy heaven, so that I may see the light of Thy glory and become attracted to Thy beauty. Verily, Thou art the Giver, the Generous, the Merciful, the Forgiving.

—*'Abdu'l-Bahá*

Family

According to the teachings of Bahá'u'lláh the family, being a human unit, must be educated according to the rules of sanctity. All the virtues must be taught the family. The integrity of the family bond must be constantly considered, and the rights of the individual members must not be transgressed. The rights of the son, the father, the mother—none of them must be transgressed, none of them must be arbitrary. Just as the son has certain obligations to his father, the father, likewise, has certain obligations to his son. The mother, the sister and other members of the household have their certain prerogatives. All these rights and prerogatives must be conserved, yet the unity of the family must be sustained. The injury of one shall be considered the injury of all; the comfort of each, the comfort of all; the honor of one, the honor of all.

—*'Abdu'l-Bahá,* The Promulgation of Universal Peace

1

I beg Thy forgiveness, O my God, and implore pardon after the manner Thou wishest Thy servants to direct themselves to Thee. I beg of Thee to wash away our sins as befitteth Thy Lordship, and to forgive me, my parents, and those who in Thy estimation have entered the abode of Thy love in a manner which is worthy of Thy transcendent sovereignty and well beseemeth the glory of Thy celestial power.

O my God! Thou hast inspired my soul to offer its supplication to Thee, and but for Thee, I would not call upon Thee. Lauded and glorified art Thou; I yield Thee praise inasmuch as Thou didst reveal Thyself unto me, and I beg Thee to forgive me, since I have fallen short in my duty to know Thee and have failed to walk in the path of Thy love.

—*The Báb*

2

O Lord! In this Most Great Dispensation Thou dost accept the intercession of children in behalf of their parents. This is one of the special infinite bestowals of this Dispensation. Therefore, O Thou kind Lord, accept the request of this Thy servant at the threshold of Thy singleness and submerge his father in the ocean of Thy grace, because this son hath arisen to render Thee service and is exerting effort at all times in the pathway of Thy love. Verily, Thou art the Giver, the Forgiver and the Kind!

—*'Abdu'l-Bahá*

3

O God, my God! This Thy handmaid is calling upon Thee, trusting in Thee, turning her face unto Thee, imploring Thee to shed Thy heavenly bounties upon her, and to disclose unto her Thy spiritual mysteries, and to cast upon her the lights of Thy Godhead.

O my Lord! Make the eyes of my husband to see. Rejoice Thou his heart with the light of the knowledge of Thee, draw Thou his mind unto Thy luminous beauty, cheer Thou his spirit by revealing unto him Thy manifest splendors.

O my Lord! Lift Thou the veil from before his sight. Rain down Thy plenteous bounties upon him, intoxicate him with the wine of love for Thee, make him one of Thy angels whose feet walk upon this earth even as their souls are soaring through the high heavens. Cause him to become a brilliant lamp, shining out with the light of Thy wisdom in the midst of Thy people. Verily, Thou art the Precious, the Ever-Bestowing, the Open of Hand.

—*'Abdu'l-Bahá*

Healing

O ye friends of God! True friends are even as skilled physicians, and the Teachings of God are as healing balm, a medicine for the conscience of man. They clear the head, so that a man can breathe them in and delight in their sweet fragrance. They waken those who sleep. They bring awareness to the unheeding, and a portion to the outcast, and to the hopeless, hope.

—*'Abdu'l-Bahá,* SELECTIONS FROM THE WRITINGS OF 'ABDU'L-BAHÁ

1

O God, my God! I beg of Thee by the ocean of Thy healing, and by the splendors of the Daystar of Thy grace, and by Thy Name through which Thou didst subdue Thy servants, and by the pervasive power of Thy most exalted Word and the potency of Thy most august Pen, and by Thy mercy that hath preceded the creation of all who are in heaven and on earth, to purge me with the waters of Thy bounty from every affliction and disorder, and from all weakness and feebleness.

Thou seest, O my Lord, Thy suppliant waiting at the door of Thy bounty, and him who hath set his hopes on Thee clinging to the cord of Thy generosity. Deny him not, I beseech Thee, the things he seeketh from the ocean of Thy grace and the Daystar of Thy loving-kindness.

Powerful art Thou to do what pleaseth Thee. There is none other God save Thee, the Ever-Forgiving, the Most Generous.

—*Bahá'u'lláh*

2

Thy name is my healing, O my God, and remembrance of Thee is my remedy. Nearness to Thee is my hope, and love for Thee is my companion. Thy mercy to me is my healing and my succor in both this world and the world to come. Thou, verily, art the All-Bountiful, the All-Knowing, the All-Wise.

—*Bahá'u'lláh*

3

Glory be to Thee, O Lord my God! I implore Thee by Thy Name, through which Thou didst lift up the ensigns of Thy guidance, and didst shed the radiance of Thy loving-kindness, and didst reveal the sovereignty of Thy Lordship; through which the lamp of Thy names hath appeared within the niche of Thine attributes, and He Who is the Tabernacle of Thy unity and the Manifestation of detachment hath shone forth; through which the ways of Thy guidance were made known, and the paths of Thy good pleasure were marked out; through which the foundations of error have been made to tremble, and the signs of wickedness have been abolished; through which the fountains of wisdom have burst forth, and the heavenly table hath been sent down; through which Thou didst preserve Thy servants and didst vouchsafe Thy healing; through which Thou didst show forth Thy tender mercies unto Thy servants and revealedst Thy forgiveness amidst Thy creatures—I implore Thee to keep safe him who hath held fast and returned unto Thee, and clung to Thy mercy, and seized the hem of Thy loving providence. Send down, then, upon him Thy healing, and make him whole, and endue him with a constancy vouchsafed by Thee, and a tranquillity bestowed by Thy highness.

Thou art, verily, the Healer, the Preserver, the Helper, the Almighty, the Powerful, the All-Glorious, the All-Knowing.

—*Bahá'u'lláh*

4

Praised be Thou, O Lord my God! I implore Thee, by Thy Most Great Name through which Thou didst stir up Thy servants and build up Thy cities, and by Thy most excellent titles, and Thy most august attributes, to assist Thy people to turn in the direction of Thy manifold bounties, and set their faces towards the Tabernacle of Thy wisdom. Heal Thou the sicknesses that have assailed the souls on every side, and have deterred them from directing their gaze towards the Paradise that lieth in the shelter of Thy shadowing Name, which Thou didst ordain to be the King of all names unto all who are in heaven and all who are on earth. Potent art Thou to do as pleaseth Thee. In Thy hands is the empire of all names. There is none other God but Thee, the Mighty, the Wise.

I am but a poor creature, O my Lord; I have clung to the hem of Thy riches. I am sore sick; I have held fast the cord of Thy healing. Deliver me from the ills that have encircled me, and wash me thoroughly with the waters of Thy graciousness and mercy, and attire me with the raiment of wholesomeness, through Thy forgiveness and bounty. Fix, then, mine eyes upon Thee, and rid me of all attachment to aught else except Thyself.

Aid me to do what Thou desirest, and to fulfill what Thou pleasest.

Thou art truly the Lord of this life and of the next. Thou art, in truth, the Ever-Forgiving, the Most Merciful.

—*Bahá'u'lláh*

5

Praise be to Thee, O Lord my God, my Master! Thou hearest the sighing of those who, though they long to behold Thy face, are yet separated from Thee and far distant from Thy court. Thou testifiest to the lamentations which those who have recognized Thee pour forth because of their exile from Thee and their yearning to meet Thee. I beseech Thee by those hearts which contain naught except the treasures of Thy remembrance and praise, and which show forth only the testimonies of Thy greatness and the evidences of Thy might, to bestow on Thy servants who desire Thee power to approach the seat of the revelation of the splendor of Thy glory and to assist them whose hopes are set on Thee to enter into the tabernacle of Thy transcendent favor and mercy.

Naked am I, O my God! Clothe me with the robe of Thy tender mercies. I am sore athirst; give me to drink of the oceans of Thy bountiful favor. I am a stranger; draw me nearer unto the source of Thy gifts. I am sick; sprinkle upon me the healing waters of Thy grace. I am a captive; rid me of my bondage, by the power of Thy might and through the force of Thy will, that I may soar on the wings of detachment towards the loftiest summits of

Thy creation. Thou, verily, doest what Thou choosest. There is no God but Thee, the Help in Peril, the All-Glorious, the Unconstrained.

—*Bahá'u'lláh*

6

For Women

Glory be to Thee, O Lord my God! I beg of Thee by Thy Name through which He Who is Thy Beauty hath been stablished upon the throne of Thy Cause, and by Thy Name through which Thou changest all things, and gatherest together all things, and callest to account all things, and rewardest all things, and preservest all things, and sustainest all things—I beg of Thee to guard this handmaiden who hath fled for refuge to Thee, and hath sought the shelter of Him in Whom Thou Thyself art manifest, and hath put her whole trust and confidence in Thee.

She is sick, O my God, and hath entered beneath the shadow of the Tree of Thy healing; afflicted, and hath fled to the City of Thy protection; diseased, and hath sought the Fountainhead of Thy favors; sorely vexed, and hath hasted to attain the Wellspring of Thy tranquillity; burdened with sin, and hath set her face toward the court of Thy forgiveness.

Attire her, by Thy sovereignty and Thy loving-kindness, O my God and my Beloved, with the raiment of Thy balm and Thy healing, and make her quaff of the cup of Thy mercy and Thy favors. Protect her, moreover, from every affliction and ailment, from all pain and sickness, and from whatsoever may be abhorrent unto Thee.

Thou, in truth, art immensely exalted above all else except Thyself. Thou art, verily, the Healer, the All-Sufficing, the Preserver, the Ever-Forgiving, the Most Merciful.

—*Bahá'u'lláh*

7

For Infants

Thou art He, O my God, through Whose names the sick are healed and the ailing are restored, and thirsty given drink and the sore vexed are tranquilized, and the wayward are guided, and the abased are exalted, and the poor are enriched, and the ignorant are enlightened, and the gloomy are illumined, and the sorrowful are cheered, and the chilled are warmed, and the downtrodden are raised up. Through Thy name, O my God, all created things were stirred up, and the heavens were spread, and the earth was established, and the clouds were raised and made to rain upon the earth. This, verily, is a token of Thy grace unto all Thy creatures.

I implore Thee, therefore, by Thy name through which Thou didst manifest Thy Godhead, and didst exalt Thy Cause above all creation, and by each of Thy most excellent titles and most august attributes, and by all the virtues wherewith Thy transcendent and most exalted Being is extolled, to send down this night from the clouds of Thy mercy the rains of Thy healing upon this suckling, whom Thou hast related unto Thine all-glorious Self in the kingdom of Thy creation. Clothe him, then, O my God, by Thy grace, with the robe of well-being and health, and guard him, O my Beloved, from every affliction and disorder, and from whatsoever is obnoxious unto Thee. Thy might, verily, is equal to all things. Thou, in truth, art the Most Powerful, the Self-Subsisting. Send down, moreover, upon him, O my God, the good of this world and of the next, and the good of the former and latter generations. Thy might and Thy wisdom are, verily, equal unto this.

—*Bahá'u'lláh*

8

The Long Healing Prayer

He is the Healer, the Sufficer, the Helper, the All-Forgiving, the All-Merciful.

I call on Thee O Exalted One, O Faithful One, O Glorious One! Thou the Sufficing, Thou the Healing, Thou the Abiding, O Thou Abiding One!

I call on Thee O Sovereign, O Upraiser, O Judge! Thou the Sufficing, Thou the Healing, Thou the Abiding, O Thou Abiding One!

I call on Thee O Peerless One, O Eternal One, O Single One! Thou the Sufficing, Thou the Healing, Thou the Abiding, O Thou Abiding One!

I call on Thee O Most Praised One, O Holy One, O Helping One! Thou the Sufficing, Thou the Healing, Thou the Abiding, O Thou Abiding One!

I call on Thee O Omniscient, O Most Wise, O Most Great One! Thou the Sufficing, Thou the Healing, Thou the Abiding, O Thou Abiding One!

I call on Thee O Clement One, O Majestic One, O Ordaining One! Thou the Sufficing, Thou the Healing, Thou the Abiding, O Thou Abiding One!

I call on Thee O Beloved One, O Cherished One, O Enraptured One! Thou the Sufficing, Thou the Healing, Thou the Abiding, O Thou Abiding One!

I call on Thee O Mightiest One, O Sustaining One, O Potent One! Thou the Sufficing, Thou the Healing, Thou the Abiding, O Thou Abiding One!

I call on Thee O Ruling One, O Self-Subsisting, O All-Knowing One! Thou the Sufficing, Thou the Healing, Thou the Abiding, O Thou Abiding One!

I call on Thee O Spirit, O Light, O Most Manifest One! Thou the Sufficing, Thou the Healing, Thou the Abiding, O Thou Abiding One!

I call on Thee O Thou Frequented by all, O Thou Known to all, O Thou Hidden from all! Thou the Sufficing, Thou the Healing, Thou the Abiding, O Thou Abiding One!

I call on Thee O Concealed One, O Triumphant One, O Bestowing One! Thou the Sufficing, Thou the Healing, Thou the Abiding, O Thou Abiding One!

I call on Thee O Almighty, O Succoring One, O Concealing One! Thou the Sufficing, Thou the Healing, Thou the Abiding, O Thou Abiding One!

I call on Thee O Fashioner, O Satisfier, O Uprooter! Thou the Sufficing, Thou the Healing, Thou the Abiding, O Thou Abiding One!

I call on Thee O Rising One, O Gathering One, O Exalting One! Thou the Sufficing, Thou the Healing, Thou the Abiding, O Thou Abiding One!

I call on Thee O Perfecting One, O Unfettered One, O Bountiful One! Thou the Sufficing, Thou the Healing, Thou the Abiding, O Thou Abiding One!

I call on Thee O Beneficent One, O Withholding One, O Creating One! Thou the Sufficing, Thou the Healing, Thou the Abiding, O Thou Abiding One!

I call on Thee O Most Sublime One, O Beauteous One, O Bounteous One! Thou the Sufficing, Thou the Healing, Thou the Abiding, O Thou Abiding One!

I call on Thee O Just One, O Gracious One, O Generous One! Thou the Sufficing, Thou the Healing, Thou the Abiding, O Thou Abiding One!

I call on Thee O All-Compelling, O Ever-Abiding, O Most Knowing One! Thou the Sufficing, Thou the Healing, Thou the Abiding, O Thou Abiding One!

I call on Thee O Magnificent One, O Ancient of Days, O Magnanimous One! Thou the Sufficing, Thou the Healing, Thou the Abiding, O Thou Abiding One!

I call on Thee O Well-Guarded One, O Lord of Joy, O Desired One! Thou the Sufficing, Thou the Healing, Thou the Abiding, O Thou Abiding One!

I call on Thee O Thou Kind to all, O Thou Compassionate with all, O Most Benevolent One! Thou the Sufficing, Thou the Healing, Thou the Abiding, O Thou Abiding One!

I call on Thee O Haven for all, O Shelter to all, O All-Preserving One! Thou the Sufficing, Thou the Healing, Thou the Abiding, O Thou Abiding One!

I call on Thee O Thou Succorer of all, O Thou Invoked by all, O Quickening One! Thou the Sufficing, Thou the Healing, Thou the Abiding, O Thou Abiding One!

I call on Thee O Unfolder, O Ravager, O Most Clement One! Thou the Sufficing, Thou the Healing, Thou the Abiding, O Thou Abiding One!

I call on Thee O Thou my Soul, O Thou my Beloved, O Thou my Faith! Thou the Sufficing, Thou the Healing, Thou the Abiding, O Thou Abiding One!

I call on Thee O Quencher of thirsts, O Transcendent Lord, O Most Precious One! Thou the Sufficing, Thou the Healing, Thou the Abiding, O Thou Abiding One!

I call on Thee O Greatest Remembrance, O Noblest Name, O Most Ancient Way! Thou the Sufficing, Thou the Healing, Thou the Abiding, O Thou Abiding One!

I call on Thee O Most Lauded, O Most Holy, O Sanctified One! Thou the Sufficing, Thou the Healing, Thou the Abiding, O Thou Abiding One!

I call on Thee O Unfastener, O Counselor, O Deliverer! Thou the Sufficing, Thou the Healing, Thou the Abiding, O Thou Abiding One!

I call on Thee O Friend, O Physician, O Captivating One! Thou the Sufficing, Thou the Healing, Thou the Abiding, O Thou Abiding One!

I call on Thee O Glory, O Beauty, O Bountiful One! Thou the Sufficing, Thou the Healing, Thou the Abiding, O Thou Abiding One!

I call on Thee O the Most Trusted, O the Best Lover, O Lord of the Dawn! Thou the Sufficing, Thou the Healing, Thou the Abiding, O Thou Abiding One!

I call on Thee O Enkindler, O Brightener, O Bringer of Delight! Thou the Sufficing, Thou the

Healing, Thou the Abiding, O Thou Abiding One!

I call on Thee O Lord of Bounty, O Most Compassionate, O Most Merciful One! Thou the Sufficing, Thou the Healing, Thou the Abiding, O Thou Abiding One!

I call on Thee O Constant One, O Life-Giving One, O Source of all Being! Thou the Sufficing, Thou the Healing, Thou the Abiding, O Thou Abiding One!

I call on Thee O Thou Who penetratest all things, O All-Seeing God, O Lord of Utterance! Thou the Sufficing, Thou the Healing, Thou the Abiding, O Thou Abiding One!

I call on Thee O Manifest yet Hidden, O Unseen yet Renowned, O Onlooker sought by all! Thou the Sufficing, Thou the Healing, Thou the Abiding, O Thou Abiding One!

I call on Thee O Thou Who slayest the Lovers, O God of Grace to the wicked!

O Sufficer, I call on Thee, O Sufficer!

O Healer, I call on Thee, O Healer!

O Abider, I call on Thee, O Abider!

Thou the Ever-Abiding, O Thou Abiding One!

Sanctified art Thou, O my God! I beseech Thee by Thy generosity, whereby the portals of Thy bounty and grace were opened wide, whereby the Temple of Thy Holiness was established upon the throne of eternity; and by Thy mercy whereby Thou didst invite all created things unto the table of Thy bounties and bestowals; and by Thy grace whereby Thou didst respond, in Thine own Self with Thy word "Yea!" on behalf of all in heaven and earth, at the hour when Thy sovereignty and Thy grandeur stood revealed, at the dawn-time when the might of Thy dominion was made manifest. And again do I beseech Thee, by these most beauteous names, by these most noble and sublime attributes, and by Thy most Exalted Remembrance, and by Thy pure and spotless Beauty, and by Thy hidden Light in the most hidden pavilion, and by Thy Name, cloaked with the garment of affliction every morn and eve, to protect the bearer of this blessed Tablet, and whoso reciteth it, and whoso cometh upon it, and whoso passeth around the house wherein it is. Heal Thou, then, by it every sick, diseased and poor one, from every tribulation and distress, from every loathsome affliction and sorrow, and guide Thou by it whosoever desireth to enter upon the paths of Thy guidance, and the ways of Thy forgiveness and grace.

Thou art verily the Powerful, the All-Sufficing, the Healing, the Protector, the Giving, the Compassionate, the All-Generous, the All-Merciful.

—*Bahá'u'lláh*

Humanity

How long will humanity persist in its waywardness? How long will injustice continue? How long is chaos and confusion to reign amongst men? How long will discord agitate the face of society? . . . The winds of despair are, alas, blowing from every direction, and the strife that divideth and afflicteth the human race is daily increasing. The signs of impending convulsions and chaos can now be discerned, inasmuch as the prevailing order appeareth to be lamentably defective. I beseech God, exalted be His glory, that He may graciously awaken the peoples of the earth, may grant that the end of their conduct may be profitable unto them, and aid them to accomplish that which beseemeth their station.

—*Bahá'u'lláh,* GLEANINGS FROM THE WRITINGS OF BAHÁ'U'LLÁH

1

My God, Whom I worship and adore! I bear witness unto Thy unity and Thy oneness, and acknowledge Thy gifts, both in the past and in the present. Thou art the All-Bountiful, the overflowing showers of Whose mercy have rained down upon high and low alike, and the splendors of Whose grace have been shed over both the obedient and the rebellious.

O God of mercy, before Whose door the quintessence of mercy hath bowed down, and round the sanctuary of Whose Cause loving-kindness, in its inmost spirit, hath circled, we beseech Thee, entreating Thine ancient grace, and seeking Thy present favor, that Thou mayest have mercy upon all who are the manifestations of the world of being, and deny them not the outpourings of Thy grace in Thy days.

All are but poor and needy, and Thou, verily, art the All-Possessing, the All-Subduing, the All-Powerful.

—*Bahá'u'lláh*

2

O Thou compassionate Lord, Thou Who art generous and able! We are servants of Thine sheltered beneath Thy providence. Cast Thy glance of favor upon us. Give light to our eyes, hearing to our ears, and understanding and love to our hearts. Render our souls joyous and happy through Thy glad tidings. O Lord! Point out to us the pathway of Thy kingdom and resuscitate all of us through the breaths of the Holy Spirit. Bestow upon us life everlasting and confer upon us never-ending honor. Unify mankind and illumine the world of humanity. May we all follow Thy pathway, long for Thy good pleasure and seek the mysteries of Thy kingdom. O God! Unite us and connect our hearts with Thy indissoluble bond. Verily, Thou art the Giver, Thou art the Kind One and Thou art the Almighty.

—*'Abdu'l-Bahá*

3

O Thou kind Lord! O Thou Who art generous and merciful! We are the servants of Thy threshold and are gathered beneath the sheltering shadow of Thy divine unity. The sun of Thy mercy is shining upon all, and the clouds of Thy bounty shower upon all. Thy gifts encompass all, Thy loving providence sustains all, Thy protection overshadows all, and the glances of Thy favor are cast upon all. O Lord! Grant Thine infinite bestowals, and let the light of Thy guidance shine. Illumine the eyes, gladden the hearts with abiding joy. Confer a new spirit upon all people and bestow upon them eternal life. Unlock the gates of true understanding and let the light of faith shine resplendent. Gather all people beneath the shadow of Thy bounty and cause them to unite in harmony, so that they may become as the rays of one sun, as the waves of one ocean, and as the fruit of one tree. May they drink from the same fountain. May they be refreshed by the same breeze. May they receive illumination from the same source of light. Thou art the Giver, the Merciful, the Omnipotent.

—'Abdu'l-Bahá

4

O Thou kind Lord! Thou hast created all humanity from the same stock. Thou hast decreed that all shall belong to the same household. In Thy Holy Presence they are all Thy servants, and all mankind are sheltered beneath Thy Tabernacle; all have gathered together at Thy Table of Bounty; all are illumined through the light of Thy Providence.

O God! Thou art kind to all, Thou hast provided for all, dost shelter all, conferrest life upon all. Thou hast endowed each and all with talents and faculties, and all are submerged in the Ocean of Thy Mercy.

O Thou kind Lord! Unite all. Let the religions agree and make the nations one, so that they may see each other as one family and the whole earth as one home. May they all live together in perfect harmony.

O God! Raise aloft the banner of the oneness of mankind.

O God! Establish the Most Great Peace.

Cement Thou, O God, the hearts together.

O Thou kind Father, God! Gladden our hearts through the fragrance of Thy love.

Brighten our eyes through the Light of Thy Guidance. Delight our ears with the melody of Thy Word, and shelter us all in the Stronghold of Thy Providence.

Thou art the Mighty and Powerful, Thou art the Forgiving and Thou art the One Who overlooketh the shortcomings of all mankind.

—*'Abdu'l-Bahá*

5

O God, O Thou Who hast cast Thy splendor over the luminous realities of men, shedding upon them the resplendent lights of knowledge and guidance, and hast chosen them out of all created things for this supernal grace, and hast caused them to encompass all things, to understand their inmost essence, and to disclose their mysteries, bringing them forth out of darkness into the visible world! "He verily showeth His special mercy to whomsoever He will."*

O Lord, help Thou Thy loved ones to acquire knowledge and the sciences and arts, and to unravel the secrets that are treasured up in the inmost reality of all created beings. Make them to hear the hidden truths that are written and embedded in the heart of all that is. Make them to be ensigns of guidance amongst all creatures, and piercing rays of the mind shedding forth their light in this, the "first life."† Make them to be leaders unto Thee, guides unto Thy path, runners urging men on to Thy Kingdom.

Thou verily art the Powerful, the Protector, the Potent, the Defender, the Mighty, the Most Generous.

—*'Abdu'l-Bahá*

* Qur'án 51:56.
† Qur'án 55:19–22.

Marriage

Bahá'í marriage is union and cordial affection between the two parties. They must, however, exercise the utmost care and become acquainted with each other's character. This eternal bond should be made secure by a firm covenant, and the intention should be to foster harmony, fellowship and unity and to attain everlasting life.

—*'Abdu'l-Bahá,* BAHÁ'Í PRAYERS

1

The pledge of marriage, the verse to be spoken individually by the bride and the bridegroom in the presence of at least two witnesses acceptable to the Spiritual Assembly is, as stipulated in the Kitáb-i-Aqdas (The Most Holy Book):

"We will all, verily, abide by the Will of God."

—*Bahá'u'lláh*

2

He is the Bestower, the Bounteous!

Praise be to God, the Ancient, the Ever-Abiding, the Changeless, the Eternal! He Who hath testified in His Own Being that verily He is the One, the Single, the Untrammeled, the Exalted. We bear witness that verily there is no God but Him, acknowledging His oneness, confessing His singleness. He hath ever dwelt in unapproachable heights, in the summits of His loftiness, sanctified from the mention of aught save Himself, free from the description of aught but Him.

And when He desired to manifest grace and beneficence to men, and to set the world in order, He revealed observances and created laws; among them He established the law of marriage, made it as a fortress for well-being and salvation, and enjoined it upon us in that which was sent down out of the heaven of sanctity in His Most Holy Book. He saith, great is His glory: "Enter into wedlock, O people, that ye may bring forth one who will make mention of Me amid My servants. This is My bidding unto you; hold fast to it as an assistance to yourselves."

—Bahá'u'lláh

3

He is God!

O peerless Lord! In Thine almighty wisdom Thou hast enjoined marriage upon the peoples, that the generations of men may succeed one another in this contingent world, and that ever, so long as the world shall last, they may busy themselves at the Threshold of Thy oneness with servitude and worship, with salutation, adoration and praise. "I have not created spirits and men, but that they should worship me."* Wherefore, wed Thou in the heaven of Thy mercy these two birds of the nest of Thy love, and make them the means of attracting perpetual grace; that from the union of these two seas of love a wave of tenderness may surge and cast the pearls of pure and goodly issue on the shore of life. "He hath let loose the two seas, that they meet each other: Between them is a barrier which they overpass not. Which then of the bounties of your Lord will ye deny? From each He bringeth up greater and lesser pearls."†

* Qur'án 3:67.

† Qur'án 56:62.

O Thou kind Lord! Make Thou this marriage to bring forth coral and pearls. Thou art verily the All-Powerful, the Most Great, the Ever-Forgiving.

—*'Abdu'l-Bahá*

4

Glory be unto Thee, O my God! Verily, this Thy servant and this Thy maidservant have gathered under the shadow of Thy mercy and they are united through Thy favor and generosity. O Lord! Assist them in this Thy world and Thy kingdom and destine for them every good through Thy bounty and grace. O Lord! Confirm them in Thy servitude and assist them in Thy service. Suffer them to become the signs of Thy Name in Thy world and protect them through Thy bestowals which are inexhaustible in this world and the world to come. O Lord! They are supplicating the kingdom of Thy mercifulness and invoking the realm of Thy singleness. Verily, they are married in obedience to Thy command. Cause them to become the signs of harmony and unity until the end of time. Verily, Thou art the Omnipotent, the Omnipresent and the Almighty!

—*'Abdu'l-Bahá*

5

O my Lord, O my Lord! These two bright orbs are wedded in Thy love, conjoined in servitude to Thy Holy Threshold, united in ministering to Thy Cause. Make Thou this marriage to be as threading lights of Thine abounding grace, O my Lord, the All-Merciful, the luminous rays of Thy bestowals, O Thou the Beneficent, the Ever-Giving, that there may branch out from this great tree boughs that will grow green and flourishing through the gifts that rain down from Thy clouds of grace.

Verily, Thou art the Generous. Verily, Thou art the Almighty. Verily, Thou art the Compassionate, the All-Merciful.

—*'Abdu'l-Bahá*

Morning

O My servants! There shineth nothing else in Mine heart except the unfading light of the Morn of Divine guidance, and out of My mouth proceedeth naught but the essence of truth, which the Lord your God hath revealed.

—*Bahá'u'lláh,* Gleanings from the Writings of Bahá'u'lláh

1

O my God and my Master! I am Thy servant and the son of Thy servant. I have risen from my couch at this dawntide when the Daystar of Thy oneness hath shone forth from the Dayspring of Thy will, and hath shed its radiance upon the whole world, according to what had been ordained in the Books of Thy Decree.

Praise be unto Thee, O my God, that we have wakened to the splendors of the light of Thy knowledge. Send down, then, upon us, O my Lord, what will enable us to dispense with anyone but Thee, and will rid us of all attachment to aught except Thyself. Write down, moreover, for me, and for such as are dear to me, and for my kindred, man and woman alike, the good of this world and the world to come. Keep us safe, then, through Thine unfailing protection, O Thou the Beloved of the entire creation and the Desire of the whole universe, from them whom Thou hast made to be the manifestations of the Evil Whisperer, who whisper in men's breasts. Potent art Thou to do Thy pleasure. Thou art, verily, the Almighty, the Help in Peril, the Self-Subsisting.

Bless Thou, O Lord my God, Him Whom Thou hast set over Thy most excellent Titles, and through Whom Thou hast divided between the godly and the wicked, and graciously aid us to do what Thou lovest and desirest. Bless Thou, moreover, O my God, them Who are Thy Words and Thy Letters, and them who have set their faces towards Thee, and turned unto Thy face, and hearkened to Thy Call.

Thou art, truly, the Lord and King of all men, and art potent over all things.

—*Bahá'u'lláh*

2

I have wakened in Thy shelter, O my God, and it becometh him that seeketh that shelter to abide within the Sanctuary of Thy protection and the Stronghold of Thy defense. Illumine my inner being, O my Lord, with the splendors of the Dayspring of Thy Revelation, even as Thou didst illumine my outer being with the morning light of Thy favor.

—Bahá'u'lláh

3

I have risen this morning by Thy grace, O my God, and left my home trusting wholly in Thee, and committing myself to Thy care. Send down, then, upon me, out of the heaven of Thy mercy, a blessing from Thy side, and enable me to return home in safety even as Thou didst enable me to set out under Thy protection with my thoughts fixed steadfastly upon Thee.

There is none other God but Thee, the One, the Incomparable, the All-Knowing, the All-Wise.

—Bahá'u'lláh

4

I give praise to Thee, O my God, that Thou hast awakened me out of my sleep, and brought me forth after my disappearance, and raised me up from my slumber. I have wakened this morning with my face set toward the splendors of the Daystar of Thy Revelation, through Which the heavens of Thy power and Thy majesty have been illumined, acknowledging Thy signs, believing in Thy Book, and holding fast unto Thy Cord.

I beseech Thee, by the potency of Thy will and the compelling power of Thy purpose, to make of what Thou didst reveal unto me in my sleep the surest foundation for the mansions of Thy love that are within the hearts of Thy loved ones, and the best instrument for the revelation of the tokens of Thy grace and Thy loving-kindness.

Do Thou ordain for me through Thy most exalted Pen, O my Lord, the good of this world and of the next. I testify that within Thy grasp are held the reins of all things. Thou changest them as Thou pleasest. No God is there save Thee, the Strong, the Faithful.

Thou art He Who changeth through His bidding abasement into glory, and weakness into strength, and powerlessness into might, and fear into calm, and doubt into certainty. No God is there but Thee, the Mighty, the Beneficent.

Thou disappointest no one who hath sought Thee, nor dost Thou keep back from Thee anyone who hath desired Thee. Ordain Thou for me what becometh the heaven of Thy generosity, and the ocean of Thy bounty. Thou art, verily, the Almighty, the Most Powerful.

—*Bahá'u'lláh*

Protection

I am He Who, from everlasting, hath been the Source of all sovereignty and power, He Who shall continue, throughout eternity, to exercise His kingship and to extend His protection unto all created things.

—*Bahá'u'lláh,* GLEANINGS FROM THE WRITINGS OF BAHÁ'U'LLÁH

1

Praise be to Thee, O Lord my God! Thou seest and knowest that I have called upon Thy servants to turn nowhere except in the direction of Thy bestowals, and have bidden them observe naught save the things Thou didst prescribe in Thy Perspicuous Book, the Book which hath been sent down according to Thine inscrutable decree and irrevocable purpose.

I can utter no word, O my God, unless I be permitted by Thee, and can move in no direction until I obtain Thy sanction. It is Thou, O my God, Who hast called me into being through the power of Thy might, and hast endued me with Thy grace to manifest Thy Cause. Wherefore I have been subjected to such adversities that my tongue hath been hindered from extolling Thee and from magnifying Thy glory.

All praise be to Thee, O my God, for the things Thou didst ordain for me through Thy decree and by the power of Thy sovereignty. I beseech Thee that Thou wilt fortify both myself and them that love me in our love for Thee, and wilt keep us firm in Thy Cause. I swear by Thy might! O my God! Thy servant's shame is to be shut out as by a veil from Thee, and his glory is to know Thee. Armed with the power of Thy name nothing can ever hurt me, and with Thy love in my heart all the world's afflictions can in no wise alarm me.

Send down, therefore, O my Lord, upon me and upon my loved ones that which will protect us from the mischief of those that have repudiated Thy truth and disbelieved in Thy signs.

Thou art, verily, the All-Glorious, the Most Bountiful.

—*Bahá'u'lláh*

2

Praised be Thou, O Lord my God! This is Thy servant who hath quaffed from the hands of Thy grace the wine of Thy tender mercy, and tasted of the savor of Thy love in Thy days. I beseech Thee, by the embodiments of Thy names whom no grief can hinder from rejoicing in Thy love or from gazing on Thy face, and whom all the hosts of the heedless are powerless to cause to turn aside from the path of Thy pleasure, to supply him with the good things Thou dost possess, and to raise him up to such heights that he will regard the world even as a shadow that vanisheth swifter than the twinkling of an eye.

Keep him safe also, O my God, by the power of Thine immeasurable majesty, from all that Thou abhorrest. Thou art, verily, his Lord and the Lord of all worlds.

—*Bahá'u'lláh*

3

Lauded be Thy name, O Lord my God! I entreat Thee by Thy Name through which the Hour hath struck, and the Resurrection came to pass, and fear and trembling seized all that are in heaven and all that are on earth, to rain down, out of the heaven of Thy mercy and the clouds of Thy tender compassion, what will gladden the hearts of Thy servants, who have turned towards Thee and helped Thy Cause.

Keep safe Thy servants and Thy handmaidens, O my Lord, from the darts of idle fancy and vain imaginings, and give them from the hands of Thy grace a draught of the soft-flowing waters of Thy knowledge.

Thou, truly, art the Almighty, the Most Exalted, the Ever-Forgiving, the Most Generous.

—*Bahá'u'lláh*

4

O God, my God! I have set out from my home, holding fast unto the cord of Thy love, and I have committed myself wholly to Thy care and Thy protection. I entreat Thee by Thy power through which Thou didst protect Thy loved ones from the wayward and the perverse, and from every contumacious oppressor, and every wicked doer who hath strayed far from Thee, to keep me safe by Thy bounty and Thy grace. Enable me, then, to return to my home by Thy power and Thy might. Thou art, truly, the Almighty, the Help in Peril, the Self-Subsisting.

—*Bahá'u'lláh*

5

In His Name, the Exalted, the All-Highest, the Most Sublime!

Glorified art Thou, O Lord my God! O Thou Who art my God, and my Master, and my Lord, and my Support, and my Hope, and my Refuge, and my Light. I ask of Thee, by Thy Hidden and Treasured Name, which none knoweth save Thine own Self, to protect the bearer of this Tablet from every calamity and pestilence, and from every wicked man and woman; from the evil of the evil-doers, and from the scheming of the unbelievers. Preserve him, moreover, O my God, from every pain and vexation, O Thou Who holdest in Thy hand the empire of all things. Thou, truly, art powerful over all things. Thou doest as Thou willest, and ordainest as Thou pleasest.

O Thou King of Kings! O Thou kind Lord! O Thou Source of ancient bounty, of grace, of generosity and bestowal! O Thou Healer of sicknesses! O Thou Sufficer of needs! O Thou Light of Light! O Thou Light above all Lights! O Thou Revealer of every Manifestation! O Thou the Compassionate! O Thou the Merciful! Do Thou have mercy upon the bearer of this Tablet, through Thy most great mercy and Thine abundant grace, O Thou the Gracious, Thou the Bounteous. Guard him, moreover, through Thy protection, from whatsoever his heart and mind may find repugnant. Of those endued with power, Thou, verily, art the most powerful. The Glory of God rest upon thee, O thou rising sun! Do thou testify unto that which God hath testified of His own Self, that there is none other God besides Him, the Almighty, the Best-Beloved.

—Bahá'u'lláh

6

Ordain for me, O my Lord, and for those who believe in Thee that which is deemed best for us in Thine estimation, as set forth in the Mother Book, for within the grasp of Thy hand Thou holdest the determined measures of all things.

Thy goodly gifts are unceasingly showered upon such as cherish Thy love, and the wondrous tokens of Thy heavenly bounties are amply bestowed on those who recognize Thy divine Unity. We commit unto Thy care whatsoever Thou hast destined for us, and implore Thee to grant us all the good that Thy knowledge embraceth.

Protect me, O my Lord, from every evil that Thine omniscience perceiveth, inasmuch as there is no power nor strength but in Thee, no triumph is forthcoming save from Thy presence, and it is Thine alone to command. Whatever God hath willed hath been, and that which He hath not willed shall not be.

There is no power nor strength except in God, the Most Exalted, the Most Mighty.

—*The Báb*

7

Glory be to Thee, O God! Thou art the God Who hath existed before all things, Who will exist after all things and will last beyond all things. Thou art the God Who knoweth all things, and is supreme over all things. Thou art the God Who dealeth mercifully with all things, Who judgeth between all things and Whose vision embraceth all things. Thou art God my Lord, Thou art aware of my position, Thou dost witness my inner and outer being.

Grant Thy forgiveness unto me and unto the believers who responded to Thy Call. Be Thou my sufficing helper against the mischief of whosoever may desire to inflict sorrow upon me or wish me ill. Verily, Thou art the Lord of all created things. Thou dost suffice everyone, while no one can be self-sufficient without Thee.

—*The Báb*

8

In the Name of God, the Lord of overpowering majesty, the All-Compelling.

Hallowed be the Lord in Whose hand is the source of dominion. He createth whatsoever He willeth by His Word of command "Be," and it is. His hath been the power of authority heretofore, and it shall remain His hereafter. He maketh victorious whomsoever He pleaseth, through the potency of His behest. He is in truth the Powerful, the Almighty. Unto Him pertaineth all glory and majesty in the kingdoms of Revelation and Creation and whatever lieth between them. Verily, He is the Potent, the All-Glorious. From everlasting He hath been the Source of indomitable strength and shall remain so unto everlasting. He is indeed the Lord of might and power. All the kingdoms of heaven and earth and whatever is between them are God's, and His power is supreme over all things. All the treasures of earth and heaven and everything between them are His, and His protection extendeth over all things. He is the Creator of the heavens and the earth and whatever lieth between them, and He truly is a witness over all things. He is the Lord of Reckoning for all that dwell in the heavens and on earth and whatever lieth between them, and truly God is swift to reckon. He setteth the measure assigned to all who are in the heavens and the earth and whatever is between them. Verily, He is the Supreme Protector. He holdeth in His grasp the keys of heaven and earth and of everything between them. At His Own pleasure doth He bestow gifts, through the power of His command. Indeed His grace encompasseth all, and He is the All-Knowing.

Say: God sufficeth unto me; He is the One Who holdeth in His grasp the kingdom of all things. Through the power of His hosts of heaven and earth and whatever lieth between them, He protecteth whomsoever among His servants He willeth. God, in truth, keepeth watch over all things.

Immeasurably exalted art Thou, O Lord! Protect us from what lieth in front of us and behind us, above our heads, on our right, on our left, below our feet and every other side to which we are exposed. Verily, Thy protection over all things is unfailing.*

—*The Báb*

* The original of this prayer for protection is written in the Báb's own hand, in the form of a pentacle.

9

O God, my God! Shield Thy trusted servants from the evils of self and passion, protect them with the watchful eye of Thy loving-kindness from all rancor, hate and envy, shelter them in the impregnable stronghold of Thy care and, safe from the darts of doubtfulness, make them the manifestations of Thy glorious signs, illumine their faces with the effulgent rays shed from the Dayspring of Thy divine unity, gladden their hearts with the verses revealed from Thy holy kingdom, strengthen their loins by Thine all-swaying power that cometh from Thy realm of glory. Thou art the All-Bountiful, the Protector, the Almighty, the Gracious.

—*'Abdu'l-Bahá*

10

O my Lord! Thou knowest that the people are encircled with pain and calamities and are environed with hardships and trouble. Every trial doth attack man and every dire adversity doth assail him like unto the assault of a serpent. There is no shelter and asylum for him except under the wing of Thy protection, preservation, guard and custody.

O Thou the Merciful One! O my Lord! Make Thy protection my armor, Thy preservation my shield, humbleness before the door of Thy oneness my guard, and Thy custody and defense my fortress and my abode. Preserve me from the suggestions of self and desire, and guard me from every sickness, trial, difficulty and ordeal.

Verily, Thou art the Protector, the Guardian, the Preserver, the Sufficer, and verily, Thou art the Merciful of the Most Merciful.

—*'Abdu'l-Bahá*

11

O Thou kind and loving Providence! The east is astir and the west surgeth even as the eternal billows of the sea. The gentle breezes of holiness are diffused and, from the Unseen Kingdom, the rays of the Orb of Truth shine forth resplendent. The anthems of divine unity are being chanted and the ensigns of celestial might are waving. The angelic Voice is raised and, even as the roaring of the leviathan, soundeth the call to selflessness and evanescence. The triumphal cry *Yá Bahá'u'l-Abhá* resoundeth on every side, and the call *Yá 'Alíyyu'l-'Alá** ringeth throughout all regions. No stir is there in the world save that of the Glory of the One Ravisher of Hearts, and no tumult is there save the surging of the love of Him, the Incomparable, the Well-Beloved.

The beloved of the Lord, with their musk-scented breath, burn like bright candles in every clime, and the friends of the All-Merciful, even as unfolding flowers, can be found in all regions. Not for a moment do they rest; they breathe not but in remembrance of Thee, and crave naught but to serve Thy Cause. In the meadows of truth they are as sweet-singing nightingales, and in the flower

* O Thou the Exalted, the Most Exalted!

garden of guidance they are even as brightly-colored blossoms. With mystic flowers they adorn the walks of the Garden of Reality; as swaying cypresses they line the riverbanks of the Divine Will. Above the horizon of being they shine as radiant stars; in the firmament of the world they gleam as resplendent orbs. Manifestations of celestial grace are they, and daysprings of the light of divine assistance.

Grant, O Thou Loving Lord, that all may stand firm and steadfast, shining with everlasting splendor, so that, at every breath, gentle breezes may blow from the bowers of Thy loving-kindness, that from the ocean of Thy grace a mist may rise, that the kindly showers of Thy love may bestow freshness, and the zephyr waft its perfume from the rose garden of divine unity.

Vouchsafe, O Best Beloved of the World, a ray from Thy Splendor. O Well-Beloved of mankind, shed upon us the light of Thy Countenance.

O God Omnipotent, do Thou shield us and be our refuge and, O Lord of Being, show forth Thy might and Thy dominion.

O Thou loving Lord, the movers of sedition are in some regions astir and active, and by night and day are inflicting a grievous wrong.

Even as wolves, tyrants are lying in wait, and the wronged, innocent flock hath neither help nor succor. Hounds are on the trail of the gazelles of the fields of divine unity, and the pheasant in the mountains of heavenly guidance is pursued by the ravens of envy.

O Thou divine Providence, preserve and protect us! O Thou Who art our Shield, save us and defend us! Keep us beneath Thy Shelter, and by Thy Help save us from all ills. Thou art, indeed, the True Protector, the Unseen Guardian, the Celestial Preserver, and the Heavenly Loving Lord.

—*'Abdu'l-Bahá*

Tests and Difficulties

Thou didst write of afflictive tests that have assailed thee. To the loyal soul, a test is but God's grace and favor; for the valiant doth joyously press forward to furious battle on the field of anguish, when the coward, whimpering with fright, will tremble and shake. So too, the proficient student, who hath with great competence mastered his subjects and committed them to memory, will happily exhibit his skills before his examiners on the day of his tests. So too will solid gold wondrously gleam and shine out in the assayer's fire.

It is clear, then, that tests and trials are, for sanctified souls, but God's bounty and grace, while to the weak, they are a calamity, unexpected and sudden.

These tests, even as thou didst write, do but cleanse the spotting of self from off the mirror of the heart, till the Sun of Truth can cast its rays thereon; for there is no veil more obstructive than the self, and however tenuous that veil may be, at the last it will completely shut a person out, and deprive him of his portion of eternal grace.

—*Abdu'l-Bahá,* SELECTIONS FROM THE WRITINGS OF 'ABDU'L-BAHÁ

1

O Thou Whose tests are a healing medicine to such as are nigh unto Thee, Whose sword is the ardent desire of all them that love Thee, Whose dart is the dearest wish of those hearts that yearn after Thee, Whose decree is the sole hope of them that have recognized Thy truth! I implore Thee, by Thy divine sweetness and by the splendors of the glory of Thy face, to send down upon us from Thy retreats on high that which will enable us to draw nigh unto Thee. Set, then, our feet firm, O my God, in Thy Cause, and enlighten our hearts with the effulgence of Thy knowledge, and illumine our breasts with the brightness of Thy names.

—Bahá'u'lláh

2

Glory to Thee, O my God! But for the tribulations which are sustained in Thy path, how could Thy true lovers be recognized; and were it not for the trials which are borne for love of Thee, how could the station of such as yearn for Thee be revealed? Thy might beareth me witness! The companions of all who adore Thee are the tears they shed, and the comforters of such as seek Thee are the groans they utter, and the food of them who haste to meet Thee is the fragments of their broken hearts.

How sweet to my taste is the bitterness of death suffered in Thy path, and how precious in my estimation are the shafts of Thine enemies when encountered for the sake of the exaltation of Thy word! Let me quaff in Thy Cause, O my God, whatsoever Thou didst desire, and send down upon me in Thy love all Thou didst ordain. By Thy glory! I wish only what Thou wishest, and cherish what Thou cherishest. In Thee have I, at all times, placed my whole trust and confidence.

Raise up, I implore Thee, O my God, as helpers to this Revelation such as shall be counted worthy of Thy name and of Thy sovereignty, that they may remember me among Thy creatures, and hoist the ensigns of Thy victory in Thy land.

Potent art Thou to do what pleaseth Thee. No God is there but Thee, the Help in Peril, the Self-Subsisting.

—*Bahá'u'lláh*

3

Glorified art Thou, O Lord my God! Every man of insight confesseth Thy sovereignty and Thy dominion, and every discerning eye perceiveth the greatness of Thy majesty and the compelling power of Thy might. The winds of tests are powerless to hold back them that enjoy near access to Thee from setting their faces towards the horizon of Thy glory, and the tempests of trials must fail to draw away and hinder such as are wholly devoted to Thy will from approaching Thy court.

Methinks, the lamp of Thy love is burning in their hearts, and the light of Thy tenderness is lit within their breasts. Adversities are incapable of estranging them from Thy Cause, and the vicissitudes of fortune can never cause them to stray from Thy pleasure.

I beseech Thee, O my God, by them and by the sighs which their hearts utter in their separation from Thee, to keep them safe from the mischief of Thine adversaries, and to nourish their souls with what Thou hast ordained for Thy loved ones on whom shall come no fear and who shall not be put to grief.

—*Bahá'u'lláh*

4

Dispel my grief by Thy bounty and Thy generosity, O God, my God, and banish mine anguish through Thy sovereignty and Thy might. Thou seest me, O my God, with my face set towards Thee at a time when sorrows have compassed me on every side. I implore Thee, O Thou Who art the Lord of all being, and overshadowest all things visible and invisible, by Thy Name whereby Thou hast subdued the hearts and the souls of men, and by the billows of the Ocean of Thy mercy and the splendors of the Daystar of Thy bounty, to number me with them whom nothing whatsoever hath deterred from setting their faces toward Thee, O Thou Lord of all names and Maker of the heavens!

Thou beholdest, O my Lord, the things which have befallen me in Thy days. I entreat Thee, by Him Who is the Dayspring of Thy names and the Dawning-Place of Thine attributes, to ordain for me what will enable me to arise to serve Thee and to extol Thy virtues. Thou art, verily, the Almighty, the Most Powerful, Who art wont to answer the prayers of all men!

And, finally, I beg of Thee by the light of Thy countenance to bless my affairs, and redeem my debts, and satisfy my needs. Thou art He to Whose power and to Whose dominion every tongue hath testified, and Whose majesty and Whose sovereignty every understanding heart hath acknowledged. No God is there but Thee, Who hearest and art ready to answer.

—*Bahá'u'lláh*

5

Lauded and glorified art Thou, O my God! I entreat Thee by the sighing of Thy lovers and by the tears shed by them that long to behold Thee, not to withhold from me Thy tender mercies in Thy Day, nor to deprive me of the melodies of the Dove that extolleth Thy oneness before the light that shineth from Thy face. I am the one who is in misery, O God! Behold me cleaving fast to Thy Name, the All-Possessing. I am the one who is sure to perish; behold me clinging to Thy Name, the Imperishable. I implore Thee, therefore, by Thy Self, the Exalted, the Most High, not to abandon me unto mine own self and unto the desires of a corrupt inclination. Hold Thou my hand with the hand of Thy power, and deliver me from the depths of my fancies and idle imaginings, and cleanse me of all that is abhorrent unto Thee.

Cause me, then, to turn wholly unto Thee, to put my whole trust in Thee, to seek Thee as my Refuge, and to flee unto Thy face. Thou art, verily, He Who, through the power of His might, doeth whatsoever He desireth, and commandeth, through the potency of His will, whatsoever He chooseth. None can withstand the operation of

Thy decree; none can divert the course of Thine appointment. Thou art, in truth, the Almighty, the All-Glorious, the Most Bountiful.

—*Bahá'u'lláh*

6

Is there any Remover of difficulties save God? Say: Praised be God! He is God! All are His servants, and all abide by His bidding!

—*The Báb*

7

Thou knowest full well, O my God, that tribulations have showered upon me from all directions and that no one can dispel or transmute them except Thee. I know of a certainty, by virtue of my love for Thee, that Thou wilt never cause tribulations to befall any soul unless Thou desirest to exalt his station in Thy celestial Paradise and to buttress his heart in this earthly life with the bulwark of Thine all-compelling power, that it may not become inclined toward the vanities of this world. Indeed Thou art well aware that under all conditions I would cherish the remembrance of Thee far more than the ownership of all that is in the heavens and on the earth.

Strengthen my heart, O my God, in Thine obedience and in Thy love, and grant that I may be clear of the entire company of Thine adversaries. Verily, I swear by Thy glory that I yearn for naught besides Thyself, nor do I desire anything except Thy mercy, nor am I apprehensive of aught save Thy justice. I beg Thee to forgive me as well as those whom Thou lovest, howsoever Thou pleasest. Verily, Thou art the Almighty, the Bountiful.

Immensely exalted art Thou, O Lord of the heavens and earth, above the praise of all men, and may peace be upon Thy faithful servants and glory be unto God, the Lord of all the worlds.

—*The Báb*

8

I adjure Thee by Thy might, O my God! Let no harm beset me in times of tests, and in moments of heedlessness guide my steps aright through Thine inspiration. Thou art God, potent art Thou to do what Thou desirest. No one can withstand Thy Will or thwart Thy Purpose.

—*The Báb*

9

O Lord! Thou art the Remover of every anguish and the Dispeller of every affliction. Thou art He Who banisheth every sorrow and setteth free every slave, the Redeemer of every soul. O Lord! Grant deliverance through Thy mercy, and reckon me among such servants of Thine as have gained salvation.

—*The Báb*

Unity

Behold the disturbances which, for many a long year, have afflicted the earth, and the perturbation that hath seized its peoples. It hath either been ravaged by war, or tormented by sudden and unforeseen calamities. Though the world is encompassed with misery and distress, yet no man hath paused to reflect what the cause or source of that may be. Whenever the True Counselor uttered a word in admonishment, lo, they all denounced Him as a mover of mischief and rejected His claim. How bewildering, how confusing is such behavior! No two men can be found who may be said to be outwardly and inwardly united. The evidences of discord and malice are apparent everywhere, though all were made for harmony and union. The Great Being saith: O well-beloved ones! The tabernacle of unity hath been raised; regard ye not one another as strangers. Ye are the fruits of one tree, and the leaves of one branch. We cherish the hope that the light of justice may shine upon the world and sanctify it from tyranny. If the rulers and kings of the earth, the symbols of the power of God, exalted be His glory, arise and resolve to dedicate themselves to whatever will promote the highest interests of the whole of humanity, the reign of justice will assuredly be established amongst the children of men, and the effulgence of its light will envelop the whole earth.

—*Bahá'u'lláh,* GLEANINGS FROM THE WRITINGS OF BAHÁ'U'LLÁH

1

O my God! O my God! Unite the hearts of Thy servants, and reveal to them Thy great purpose. May they follow Thy commandments and abide in Thy law. Help them, O God, in their endeavor, and grant them strength to serve Thee. O God! Leave them not to themselves, but guide their steps by the light of Thy knowledge, and cheer their hearts by Thy love. Verily, Thou art their Helper and their Lord.

—*Bahá'u'lláh*

2

O my God! O my God! Verily, I invoke Thee and supplicate before Thy threshold, asking Thee that all Thy mercies may descend upon these souls. Specialize them for Thy favor and Thy truth.

O Lord! Unite and bind together the hearts, join in accord all the souls, and exhilarate the spirits through the signs of Thy sanctity and oneness. O Lord! Make these faces radiant through the light of Thy oneness. Strengthen the loins of Thy servants in the service of Thy kingdom.

O Lord, Thou possessor of infinite mercy! O Lord of forgiveness and pardon! Forgive our sins, pardon our shortcomings, and cause us to turn to the kingdom of Thy clemency, invoking the kingdom of might and power, humble at Thy shrine and submissive before the glory of Thine evidences.

O Lord God! Make us as waves of the sea, as flowers of the garden, united, agreed through the bounties of Thy love. O Lord! Dilate the breasts through the signs of Thy oneness, and make all mankind as stars shining from the same height of glory, as perfect fruits growing upon Thy tree of life.

Verily, Thou art the Almighty, the Self-Subsistent, the Giver, the Forgiving, the Pardoner, the Omniscient, the One Creator.

—*'Abdu'l-Bahá*

Women

In proclaiming the oneness of mankind He taught that men and women are equal in the sight of God and that there is no distinction to be made between them. The only difference between them now is due to lack of education and training. If woman is given equal opportunity of education, distinction and estimate of inferiority will disappear. The world of humanity has two wings, as it were: One is the female; the other is the male. If one wing be defective, the strong perfect wing will not be capable of flight. The world of humanity has two hands. If one be imperfect, the capable hand is restricted and unable to perform its duties. God is the Creator of mankind. He has endowed both sexes with perfections and intelligence, given them physical members and organs of sense, without differentiation or distinction as to superiority; therefore, why should woman be considered inferior? This is not according to the plan and justice of God. He has created them equal; in His estimate there is no question of sex.

The one whose heart is purest, whose deeds are most perfect, is acceptable to God, male or female.

—*'Abdu'l-Bahá,* THE PROMULGATION OF UNIVERSAL PEACE

1

O Thou Whose face is the object of the adoration of all that yearn after Thee, Whose presence is the hope of such as are wholly devoted to Thy will, Whose nearness is the desire of all that have drawn nigh unto Thy court, Whose countenance is the companion of those who have recognized Thy truth, Whose name is the mover of the souls that long to behold Thy face, Whose voice is the true life of Thy lovers, the words of Whose mouth are as the waters of life unto all who are in heaven and on earth!

I beseech Thee, by the wrong Thou hast suffered and the ills inflicted upon Thee by the hosts of wrongful doers, to send down upon me from the clouds of Thy mercy that which will purify me of all that is not of Thee, that I may be worthy to praise Thee and fit to love Thee.

Withhold not from me, O my Lord, the things Thou didst ordain for such of Thy handmaidens as circle around Thee, and on whom are poured continually the splendors of the sun of Thy beauty and the beams of the brightness of Thy face. Thou art He Who from everlasting hath succored whosoever hath sought Thee, and bountifully favored him who hath asked Thee.

No God is there beside Thee, the Mighty, the Ever-Abiding, the All-Bounteous, the Most Generous.

—*Bahá'u'lláh*

2

Glory be to Thee, O my God! My face hath been set towards Thy face, and my face is, verily, Thy face, and my call is Thy call, and my Revelation Thy Revelation, and my self Thy Self, and my Cause Thy Cause, and my behest Thy behest, and my Being Thy Being, and my sovereignty Thy sovereignty, and my glory Thy glory, and my power Thy power.

I implore Thee, O Thou Fashioner of the nations and the King of eternity, to guard Thy handmaidens within the tabernacle of Thy chastity, and to cancel such of their deeds as are unworthy of Thy days. Purge out, then, from them, O my God, all doubts and idle fancies, and sanctify them from whatsoever becometh not their kinship with Thee, O Thou Who art the Lord of names, and the Source of utterance. Thou art He in Whose grasp are the reins of the entire creation.

No God is there but Thee, the Almighty, the Most Exalted, the All-Glorious, the Self-Subsisting.

—*Bahá'u'lláh*

3

Glorified art Thou, O Lord my God! Thou art He the fire of Whose love hath set ablaze the hearts of them who have recognized Thy unity, and the splendors of Whose countenance have illuminated the faces of such as have drawn nigh unto Thy court. How plenteous, O my God, is the stream of Thy knowledge! How sweet, O my Beloved, is the injury which, in my love for Thee, and for the sake of Thy pleasure, I suffer from the darts of the wicked doers! How pleasing are the wounds which, in Thy path and in order to proclaim Thy Faith, I sustain from the swords of the infidels!

I beseech Thee, by Thy name through which Thou turnest restlessness into tranquillity, fear into confidence, weakness into strength, and abasement into glory, that Thou of Thy grace wilt aid me and Thy servants to exalt Thy name, to deliver Thy Message, and to proclaim Thy Cause, in such wise that we may remain unmoved by either the assaults of the transgressors or the wrath of the infidels, O Thou Who art my Well-Beloved!

I am, O my Lord, Thy handmaiden, who hath hearkened to Thy call, and hastened unto Thee, fleeing from herself and resting her heart upon Thee. I implore Thee, O my Lord, by Thy name out of which all the treasures of the earth were brought forth, to shield me from the hints of such as have disbelieved in Thee and repudiated Thy truth.

Powerful art Thou to do what Thou pleasest. Thou art, verily, the All-Knowing, the All-Wise.

—*Bahá'u'lláh*

4

Magnified be Thy name, O Lord my God! Behold Thou mine eye expectant to gaze on the wonders of Thy mercy, and mine ear longing to hearken unto Thy sweet melodies, and my heart yearning for the living waters of Thy knowledge. Thou seest Thy handmaiden, O my God, standing before the habitation of Thy mercy, and calling upon Thee by Thy name which Thou hast chosen above all other names and set up over all that are in heaven and on earth. Send down upon her the breaths of Thy mercy, that she may be carried away wholly from herself, and be drawn entirely towards the seat which, resplendent with the glory of Thy face, sheddeth afar the radiance of Thy sovereignty, and is established as Thy throne. Potent art Thou to do what Thou willest. No God is there beside Thee, the All-Glorious, the Most Bountiful.

Cast not out, I entreat Thee, O my Lord, them that have sought Thee, and turn not away such as have directed their steps towards Thee, and deprive not of Thy grace all that love Thee. Thou art He, O my Lord, Who hath called Himself the God of Mercy, the Most Compassionate. Have mercy, then, upon Thy handmaiden who hath sought Thy shelter, and set her face towards Thee.

Thou art, verily, the Ever-Forgiving, the Most Merciful.

—Bahá'u'lláh

5

O Thou, at Whose dreadful majesty all things have trembled, in Whose grasp are the affairs of all men, towards Whose grace and mercy are set the faces of all Thy creatures! I entreat Thee, by Thy Name which Thou hast ordained to be the spirit of all names that are in the kingdom of names, to shield us from the whisperings of those who have turned away from Thee, and have repudiated the truth of Thy most august and most exalted Self, in this Revelation that hath caused the kingdom of Thy names to tremble.

I am one of Thy handmaidens, O my Lord! I have turned my face towards the sanctuary of Thy gracious favors and the adored tabernacle of Thy glory. Purify me of all that is not of Thee, and strengthen me to love Thee and to fulfill Thy pleasure, that I may delight myself in the contemplation of Thy beauty, and be rid of all attachment to any of Thy creatures, and may, at every moment, proclaim: "Magnified be God, the Lord of the worlds!"

Let my food, O my Lord, be Thy beauty, and my drink the light of Thy presence, and my hope Thy pleasure, and my work Thy praise, and my companion Thy remembrance, and my aid Thy sovereignty, and my dwelling-place Thy habitation, and my home the seat which Thou hast exalted above the limitations of them that are shut out as by a veil from Thee.

Thou art, in truth, the God of power, of strength and glory.

—*Bahá'u'lláh*

6

Glory to Thee, O my God! One of Thy handmaidens, who hath believed in Thee and in Thy signs, hath entered beneath the shadow of the tree of Thy oneness. Give her to quaff, O my God, by Thy Name, the Manifest and the Hidden, of Thy choice sealed Wine that it may take her away from her own self, and make her to be entirely devoted to Thy remembrance, and wholly detached from any one beside Thee.

Now that Thou hast revealed unto her the knowledge of Thee, O my Lord, deny her not, by Thy bounty, Thy grace; and now that Thou hast called her unto Thyself, drive her not away from Thee, through Thy favor. Supply her, then, with that which excelleth all that can be found on Thine earth. Thou art, verily, the Most Bountiful, Whose grace is immense.

Wert Thou to bestow on one of Thy creatures what would equal the kingdoms of earth and heaven, it would still not diminish by even as much as an atom the immensity of Thy dominion. Far greater art Thou than the Great One men are wont to call Thee, for such a title is but one of Thy names all of which were created by a mere indication of Thy will.

There is no God but Thee, the God of power, the God of glory, the God of knowledge and wisdom.

—*Bahá'u'lláh*

7

Thou seest, O my God, how the wrongs committed by such of Thy creatures as have turned their backs to Thee have come in between Him in Whom Thy Godhead is manifest and Thy servants. Send down upon them, O my Lord, what will cause them to be busied with each others' concerns. Let, then, their violence be confined to their own selves, that the land and they that dwell therein may find peace.

One of Thy handmaidens, O my Lord, hath sought Thy face, and soared in the atmosphere of Thy pleasure. Withhold not from her, O my Lord, the things Thou didst ordain for the chosen ones among Thy handmaidens. Enable her, then, to be so attracted by Thine utterances that she will celebrate Thy praise amongst them.

Potent art Thou to do what pleaseth Thee. No God is there but Thee, the Almighty, Whose help is implored by all men.

—*Bahá'u'lláh*

8

O my Lord, my Beloved, my Desire! Befriend me in my loneliness and accompany me in my exile. Remove my sorrow. Cause me to be devoted to Thy beauty. Withdraw me from all else save Thee. Attract me through Thy fragrances of holiness. Cause me to be associated in Thy Kingdom with those who are severed from all else save Thee, who long to serve Thy sacred threshold and who stand to work in Thy Cause. Enable me to be one of Thy maidservants who have attained to Thy good pleasure. Verily, Thou art the Gracious, the Generous.

—*'Abdu'l-Bahá*

9

Expectant Mothers

My Lord! My Lord! I praise Thee and I thank Thee for that whereby Thou hast favored Thine humble maidservant, Thy slave beseeching and supplicating Thee, because Thou hast verily guided her unto Thine obvious Kingdom and caused her to hear Thine exalted Call in the contingent world and to behold Thy Signs which prove the appearance of Thy victorious reign over all things.

O my Lord, I dedicate that which is in my womb unto Thee. Then cause it to be a praiseworthy child in Thy Kingdom and a fortunate one by Thy favor and Thy generosity; to develop and to grow up under the charge of Thine education. Verily, Thou art the Gracious! Verily, Thou art the Lord of Great Favor!

—*'Abdu'l-Bahá*

Youth

O loved ones of 'Abdu'l-Bahá!

Man's life has its springtime and is endowed with marvelous glory. The period of youth is characterized by strength and vigor and stands out as the choicest time in human life. Therefore you should strive day and night so that endowed with heavenly strength, inspired with brilliant motives and aided by His celestial power and heavenly grace and confirmation, you may become the ornaments of the world of humanity, and preeminent among those who are initiated into true learning and the love of God. You must be distinguished amidst men by your sanctity and detachment, loftiness of purpose, magnanimity, determination, noble-mindedness, tenacity, the elevation of your aims and your spiritual qualities; that you may become the means of exaltation and glory for the Cause of God and the dawning places of His heavenly bestowals.

—*'Abdu'l-Bahá,* O GOD, MY GOD . . .
BAHÁ'Í PRAYERS AND TABLETS FOR CHILDREN AND YOUTH

1

O Thou kind Lord! From the horizon of detachment Thou hast manifested souls that, even as the shining moon, shed radiance upon the realm of heart and soul, rid themselves from the attributes of the world of existence and hastened forth unto the kingdom of immortality. With a drop from the ocean of Thy loving-kindness Thou didst oft-times moisten the gardens of their hearts until they gained incomparable freshness and beauty. The holy fragrance of Thy divine unity was diffused far and wide, shedding its sweet savors over the entire world, causing the regions of the earth to be redolent with perfume.

Raise up then, O spirit of Purity, souls who, like those sanctified beings, will become free and pure, will adorn the world of being with a new raiment and a wondrous robe, will seek no one else but Thee, tread no path except the path of Thy good pleasure and will speak of naught but the mysteries of Thy Cause.

O Thou kind Lord! Grant that this youth may attain unto that which is the highest aspiration of the holy ones. Endow him with the wings of Thy strengthening grace—wings of detachment and divine aid—that he may soar thereby into the atmosphere of Thy tender mercy, be able to partake of Thy celestial bestowals, may become a sign of divine guidance and a standard of the Concourse on high. Thou art the Potent, the Powerful, the Seeing, the Hearing.

—*'Abdu'l-Bahá*

2

O Thou kind Lord! Graciously bestow a pair of heavenly wings unto each of these fledglings, and give them spiritual power that they may wing their flight through this limitless space and may soar to the heights of the Abhá Kingdom.

O Lord! Strengthen these fragile seedlings that each one may become a fruitful tree, verdant and flourishing. Render these souls victorious through the potency of Thy celestial hosts, that they may be able to crush the forces of error and ignorance and to unfurl the standard of fellowship and guidance amidst the people; that they may, even as the reviving breaths of the spring, refresh and quicken the trees of human souls and like unto vernal showers make the meads of that region green and fertile.

Thou art the Mighty and the Powerful; Thou art the Bestower and the All-Loving.

—*'Abdu'l-Bahá*

3

O Thou kind Lord! Bestow heavenly confirmation upon this daughter of the kingdom, and graciously aid her that she may remain firm and steadfast in Thy Cause and that she may, even as a nightingale of the rose garden of mysteries, warble melodies in the Abhá Kingdom in the most wondrous tones, thereby bringing happiness to everyone. Make her exalted among the daughters of the kingdom and enable her to attain life eternal.

Thou art the Bestower, the All-Loving.

—*'Abdu'l-Bahá*

4

O Lord! Make this youth radiant, and confer Thy bounty upon this poor creature. Bestow upon him knowledge, grant him added strength at the break of every morn and guard him within the shelter of Thy protection so that he may be freed from error, may devote himself to the service of Thy Cause, may guide the wayward, lead the hapless, free the captives and awaken the heedless, that all may be blessed with Thy remembrance and praise. Thou art the Mighty and the Powerful.

—*'Abdu'l-Bahá*

5

Praise and glory be to Thee, O Lord my God! This is a choice sapling which Thou hast planted in the meads of Thy love and hast nurtured with the fingers of Thy Lordship. Thou hast watered it from the wellspring of everlasting life which streameth forth from the gardens of Thy oneness and Thou hast caused the clouds of Thy tender mercy to shower Thy favors upon it. It hath now grown and developed beneath the shelter of Thy blessings which are manifest from the Dayspring of Thy divine essence. It hath burst forth into leaves and blossoms, is laden with fruit through the providence of Thy wondrous gifts and bounties and is stirred by the fragrant breeze wafting from the direction of Thy loving-kindness.

O Lord! Cause this sapling to become verdant, fresh and flourishing by the outpourings of Thy special bounty and favor, wherewith Thou hast endued the tabernacles of holiness in Thy eternal Kingdom and hast adorned the essences of unity in the arena of reunion.

O Lord! Assist him through Thy strengthening grace which proceedeth from Thine invisible Kingdom, aid him with such hosts as are hidden from the eyes of Thy servants and grant that he may have a sure footing in Thy presence. Unloose his tongue to make mention of Thee and gladden his heart to celebrate Thy praise. Illumine his face in Thy Kingdom, prosper him in the realm above and graciously confirm him to serve Thy Cause.

Thou art the All-Powerful, the All-Glorious, the Omnipotent.

—'Abdu'l-Bahá

III

SELECTIONS FROM THE WRITINGS OF BAHÁ'U'LLÁH AND 'ABDU'L-BAHÁ

Tablet of Aḥmad

According to Shoghi Effendi, the Guardian of the Bahá'í Faith, the Tablet of Aḥmad was "invested by Bahá'u'lláh with a special potency and significance." Bahá'ís often recite this tablet during times of extreme hardship. For clarification, the word *Bayán* in the fifth paragraph refers to the book of laws and exhortations revealed by the Báb, Who was Bahá'u'lláh's Forerunner. Bahá'u'lláh revealed this tablet in 1865 in honor of a man named Aḥmad, who was one of His devoted followers.*

---

* Shoghi Effendi, in *Bahá'í Prayers*, p. 307; Taherzadeh, *Revelation of Bahá'u'lláh*, 2:111–13.

Tablet of Aḥmad

He is the King, the All-Knowing, the Wise! Lo, the Nightingale of Paradise singeth upon the twigs of the Tree of Eternity, with holy and sweet melodies, proclaiming to the sincere ones the glad tidings of the nearness of God, calling the believers in the Divine Unity to the court of the Presence of the Generous One, informing the severed ones of the message which hath been revealed by God, the King, the Glorious, the Peerless, guiding the lovers to the seat of sanctity and to this resplendent Beauty.

Verily this is that Most Great Beauty, foretold in the Books of the Messengers, through Whom truth shall be distinguished from error and the wisdom of every command shall be tested. Verily He is the Tree of Life that bringeth forth the fruits of God, the Exalted, the Powerful, the Great.

O Aḥmad! Bear thou witness that verily He is God and there is no God but Him, the King, the Protector, the Incomparable, the Omnipotent. And that the One Whom He hath sent forth by the name of 'Alí* was the true One from God, to Whose commands we are all conforming.

Say: O people be obedient to the ordinances of God, which have been enjoined in the Bayán by

---

* The Báb.

the Glorious, the Wise One. Verily He is the King of the Messengers and His Book is the Mother Book did ye but know. Thus doth the Nightingale utter His call unto you from this prison. He hath but to deliver this clear message. Whosoever desireth, let him turn aside from this counsel and whosoever desireth let him choose the path to his Lord.

O people, if ye deny these verses, by what proof have ye believed in God? Produce it, O assemblage of false ones. Nay, by the One in Whose hand is my soul, they are not, and never shall be able to do this, even should they combine to assist one another.

O Aḥmad! Forget not My bounties while I am absent. Remember My days during thy days, and My distress and banishment in this remote prison. And be thou so steadfast in My love that thy heart shall not waver, even if the swords of the enemies rain blows upon thee and all the heavens and the earth arise against thee.

Be thou as a flame of fire to My enemies and a river of life eternal to My loved ones, and be not of those who doubt.

And if thou art overtaken by affliction in My path, or degradation for My sake, be not thou troubled thereby.

Rely upon God, thy God and the Lord of thy fathers. For the people are wandering in the paths of delusion, bereft of discernment to see God with their own eyes, or hear His Melody with their own ears. Thus have We found them, as thou also dost witness.

Thus have their superstitions become veils between them and their own hearts and kept them from the path of God, the Exalted, the Great.

Be thou assured in thyself that verily, he who turneth away from this Beauty hath also turned away from the Messengers of the past and showeth pride towards God from all eternity to all eternity.

Learn well this Tablet, O Aḥmad. Chant it during thy days and withhold not thyself therefrom. For verily, God hath ordained for the one who chants it, the reward of a hundred martyrs and a service in both worlds. These favors have We bestowed upon thee as a bounty on Our part and a mercy from Our presence, that thou mayest be of those who are grateful.

By God! Should one who is in affliction or grief read this Tablet with absolute sincerity, God will dispel his sadness, solve his difficulties and remove his afflictions.

Verily, He is the Merciful, the Compassionate. Praise be to God, the Lord of all the worlds.

—*Bahá'u'lláh*

Fire Tablet

Bahá'u'lláh revealed the Fire Tablet in late 1871 in response to a letter written to Him by a Bahá'í named Hájí Siyyid 'Ali-Akbar-i-Dahájí—hence the address at the end of the tablet that reads, "O 'Alí-Akbar, thank thy Lord for this Tablet . . ." In this tablet, Bahá'u'lláh describes some of the great suffering He was made to endure during His lifetime. Bahá'ís often recite this tablet during times of difficulty and hardship.*

* Taherzadeh, *Revelation of Bahá'u'lláh,* 3:226.

Fire Tablet

In the Name of God, the Most Ancient, the Most Great.

Indeed the hearts of the sincere are consumed in the fire of separation: Where is the gleaming of the light of Thy Countenance, O Beloved of the worlds?

Those who are near unto Thee have been abandoned in the darkness of desolation: Where is the shining of the morn of Thy reunion, O Desire of the worlds?

The bodies of Thy chosen ones lie quivering on distant sands: Where is the ocean of Thy presence, O Enchanter of the worlds?

Longing hands are uplifted to the heaven of Thy grace and generosity: Where are the rains of Thy bestowal, O Answerer of the worlds?

The infidels have arisen in tyranny on every hand: Where is the compelling power of Thine ordaining pen, O Conqueror of the worlds?

The barking of dogs is loud on every side: Where is the lion of the forest of Thy might, O Chastiser of the worlds?

Coldness hath gripped all mankind: Where is the warmth of Thy love, O Fire of the worlds?

Calamity hath reached its height: Where are the signs of Thy succor, O Salvation of the worlds?

Darkness hath enveloped most of the peoples: Where is the brightness of Thy splendor, O Radiance of the worlds?

The necks of men are stretched out in malice: Where are the swords of Thy vengeance, O Destroyer of the worlds?

Abasement hath reached its lowest depth: Where are the emblems of Thy glory, O Glory of the worlds?

Sorrows have afflicted the Revealer of Thy Name, the All-Merciful: Where is the joy of the Dayspring of Thy Revelation, O Delight of the worlds?

Anguish hath befallen all the peoples of the earth: Where are the ensigns of Thy gladness, O Joy of the worlds?

Thou seest the Dawning Place of Thy signs veiled by evil suggestions: Where are the fingers of Thy might, O Power of the worlds?

Sore thirst hath overcome all men: Where is the river of Thy bounty, O Mercy of the worlds?

Greed hath made captive all mankind: Where are the embodiments of detachment, O Lord of the worlds?

Thou seest this Wronged One lonely in exile: Where are the hosts of the heaven of Thy Command, O Sovereign of the worlds?

I have been forsaken in a foreign land: Where are the emblems of Thy faithfulness, O Trust of the worlds?

The agonies of death have laid hold on all men: Where is the surging of Thine ocean of eternal life, O Life of the worlds?

The whisperings of Satan have been breathed to every creature: Where is the meteor of Thy fire, O Light of the worlds?

The drunkenness of passion hath perverted most of mankind: Where are the daysprings of purity, O Desire of the worlds?

Thou seest this Wronged One veiled in tyranny among the Syrians: Where is the radiance of Thy dawning light, O Light of the worlds?

Thou seest Me forbidden to speak forth: Then from where will spring Thy melodies, O Nightingale of the worlds?

Most of the people are enwrapped in fancy and idle imaginings: Where are the exponents of Thy certitude, O Assurance of the worlds?

Bahá is drowning in a sea of tribulation: Where is the Ark of Thy salvation, O Savior of the worlds?

Thou seest the Dayspring of Thine utterance in the darkness of creation: Where is the sun of the heaven of Thy grace, O Light-Giver of the worlds?

The lamps of truth and purity, of loyalty and honor, have been put out: Where are the signs of Thine avenging wrath, O Mover of the worlds?

Canst Thou see any who have championed Thy Self, or who ponder on what hath befallen Him in the pathway of Thy love? Now doth My pen halt, O Beloved of the worlds.

The branches of the Divine Lote-Tree lie broken by the onrushing gales of destiny: Where are the banners of Thy succor, O Champion of the worlds?

This Face is hidden in the dust of slander: Where are the breezes of Thy compassion, O Mercy of the worlds?

The robe of sanctity is sullied by the people of deceit: Where is the vesture of Thy holiness, O Adorner of the worlds?

The sea of grace is stilled for what the hands of men have wrought: Where are the waves of Thy bounty, O Desire of the worlds?

The door leading to the Divine Presence is locked through the tyranny of Thy foes: Where is the key of Thy bestowal, O Unlocker of the worlds?

The leaves are yellowed by the poisoning winds of sedition: Where is the downpour of the clouds of Thy bounty, O Giver of the worlds?

The universe is darkened with the dust of sin: Where are the breezes of Thy forgiveness, O Forgiver of the worlds?

This Youth is lonely in a desolate land: Where is the rain of Thy heavenly grace, O Bestower of the worlds?

O Supreme Pen, We have heard Thy most sweet call in the eternal realm: Give Thou ear unto what the Tongue of Grandeur uttereth, O Wronged One of the worlds!

Were it not for the cold, how would the heat of Thy words prevail, O Expounder of the worlds?

Were it not for calamity, how would the sun of Thy patience shine, O Light of the worlds? Lament not because of the wicked. Thou wert created to bear and endure, O Patience of the worlds.

How sweet was Thy dawning on the horizon of the Covenant among the stirrers of sedition, and Thy yearning after God, O Love of the worlds.

By Thee the banner of independence was planted on the highest peaks, and the sea of bounty surged, O Rapture of the worlds.

By Thine aloneness the Sun of Oneness shone, and by Thy banishment the land of Unity was adorned. Be patient, O Thou Exile of the worlds.

We have made abasement the garment of glory, and affliction the adornment of Thy temple, O Pride of the worlds.

Thou seest the hearts are filled with hate, and to overlook is Thine, O Thou Concealer of the sins of the worlds.

When the swords flash, go forward! When the shafts fly, press onward! O Thou Sacrifice of the worlds.

Dost Thou wail, or shall I wail? Rather shall I weep at the fewness of Thy champions, O Thou Who hast caused the wailing of the worlds.

Verily, I have heard Thy Call, O All-Glorious Beloved; and now is the face of Bahá flaming with the heat of tribulation and with the fire of Thy shining word, and He hath risen up in faithfulness at the place of sacrifice, looking toward Thy pleasure, O Ordainer of the worlds.

O 'Alí-Akbar, thank thy Lord for this Tablet whence thou canst breathe the fragrance of My meekness, and know what hath beset Us in the path of God, the Adored of all the worlds.

Should all the servants read and ponder this, there shall be kindled in their veins a fire that shall set aflame the worlds.

—Bahá'u'lláh

Tablet of the Holy Mariner

Bahá'u'lláh revealed the Tablet of the Holy Mariner on the fifth day of Naw-Rúz (Persian New Year) in 1863 while He was staying on the outskirts of Baghdad. Shortly after this tablet was revealed, the government of the Ottoman Empire ordered Bahá'u'lláh to leave Baghdad with His family and travel to Constantinople, the capital of the Ottoman Empire. The theme of this tablet is the necessity of being faithful to the Covenant of God* at all times.† The term *Blessed Beauty*, in the epigraph by 'Abdu'l-Bahá, refers to Bahá'u'lláh.

* According to Bahá'u'lláh, God has promised to always guide and instruct humanity through a series of Divine Messengers, Whom humanity has the obligation to accept and obey.

† Taherzadeh, *Revelation of Bahá'u'lláh*, 1:229–30.

Tablet of the Holy Mariner

"Study the Tablet of the Holy Mariner that ye may know the truth, and consider that the Blessed Beauty hath fully foretold future events. Let them who perceive, take warning!"

—*'Abdu'l-Bahá*

He is the Gracious, the Well-Beloved!
O Holy Mariner!
Bid thine ark of eternity appear before the Celestial Concourse,
Glorified be my Lord, the All-Glorious!
Launch it upon the ancient sea, in His Name, the Most Wondrous,
Glorified be my Lord, the All-Glorious!
And let the angelic spirits enter, in the Name of God, the Most High.
Glorified be my Lord, the All-Glorious!
Unmoor it, then, that it may sail upon the ocean of glory,
Glorified be my Lord, the All-Glorious!
Haply the dwellers therein may attain the retreats of nearness in the everlasting realm.
Glorified be my Lord, the All-Glorious!
Having reached the sacred strand, the shore of the crimson seas,

Glorified be my Lord, the All-Glorious!

Bid them issue forth and attain this ethereal invisible station,

Glorified be my Lord, the All-Glorious!

A station wherein the Lord hath in the Flame of His Beauty appeared within the deathless tree;

Glorified be my Lord, the All-Glorious!

Wherein the embodiments of His Cause cleansed themselves of self and passion;

Glorified be my Lord, the All-Glorious!

Around which the Glory of Moses doth circle with the everlasting hosts;

Glorified be my Lord, the All-Glorious!

Wherein the Hand of God was drawn forth from His bosom of Grandeur;

Glorified be my Lord, the All-Glorious!

Wherein the ark of the Cause remaineth motionless even though to its dwellers be declared all divine attributes.

Glorified be my Lord, the All-Glorious!

O Mariner! Teach them that are within the ark that which we have taught thee behind the mystic veil.

Glorified be my Lord, the All-Glorious!

Perchance they may not tarry in the sacred snow-white spot,

Glorified be my Lord, the All-Glorious!

But may soar upon the wings of the spirit unto that station which the Lord hath exalted above all mention in the worlds below,

Glorified be my Lord, the All-Glorious!

May wing through space even as the favored birds in the realm of eternal reunion;

Glorified be my Lord, the All-Glorious!

May know the mysteries hidden in the Seas of light.

Glorified be my Lord, the All-Glorious!

They passed the grades of worldly limitations and reached that of the divine unity, the center of heavenly guidance.

Glorified be my Lord, the All-Glorious!

They have desired to ascend unto that state which the Lord hath ordained to be above their stations.

Glorified be my Lord, the All-Glorious!

Whereupon the burning meteor cast them out from them that abide in the Kingdom of His Presence,

Glorified be my Lord, the All-Glorious!

And they heard the Voice of Grandeur raised from behind the unseen pavilion upon the

Height of Glory:

Glorified be my Lord, the All-Glorious!

"O guardian angels! Return them to their abode in the world below,

Glorified be my Lord, the All-Glorious!

"Inasmuch as they have purposed to rise to that sphere which the wings of the celestial dove have never attained;

Glorified be my Lord, the All-Glorious!

"Whereupon the ship of fancy standeth still which the minds of them that comprehend cannot grasp."

Glorified be my Lord, the All-Glorious!

Whereupon the maid of heaven looked out from her exalted chamber,

Glorified be my Lord, the All-Glorious!

And with her brow signed to the Celestial Concourse,

Glorified be my Lord, the All-Glorious!

Flooding with the light of her countenance the heaven and the earth,

Glorified be my Lord, the All-Glorious!

And as the radiance of her beauty shone upon the people of dust,

Glorified be my Lord, the All-Glorious!

All beings were shaken in their mortal graves.

Glorified be my Lord, the All-Glorious!

She then raised the call which no ear through all eternity hath ever heard,

Glorified be my Lord, the All-Glorious!

And thus proclaimed: "By the Lord! He whose heart hath not the fragrance of the love of the exalted and glorious Arabian Youth,

Glorified be my Lord, the All-Glorious!

"Can in no wise ascend unto the glory of the highest heaven."

Glorified be my Lord, the All-Glorious!

Thereupon she summoned unto herself one maiden from her handmaidens,

Glorified be my Lord, the All-Glorious!

And commanded her: "Descend into space from the mansions of eternity,

Glorified be my Lord, the All-Glorious!

"And turn thou unto that which they have concealed in the inmost of their hearts.

Glorified be my Lord, the All-Glorious!

"Shouldst thou inhale the perfume of the robe from the Youth that hath been hidden within the tabernacle of light by reason of that which the hands of the wicked have wrought,

Glorified be my Lord, the All-Glorious!

"Raise a cry within thyself, that all the inmates of the chambers of Paradise, that are the embodiments of the eternal wealth, may understand and hearken;

Glorified be my Lord, the All-Glorious!

"That they may all come down from their everlasting chambers and tremble,

Glorified be my Lord, the All-Glorious!

"And kiss their hands and feet for having soared to the heights of faithfulness;

Glorified be my Lord, the All-Glorious!

"Perchance they may find from their robes the fragrance of the Beloved One."

Glorified be my Lord, the All-Glorious!

Thereupon the countenance of the favored damsel beamed above the celestial chambers

even as the light that shineth from the face of the Youth above His mortal temple;

Glorified be my Lord, the All-Glorious!

She then descended with such an adorning as to illumine the heavens and all that is therein.

Glorified be my Lord, the All-Glorious!

She bestirred herself and perfumed all things in the lands of holiness and grandeur.

Glorified be my Lord, the All-Glorious!

When she reached that place she rose to her full height in the midmost heart of creation,

Glorified be my Lord, the all-Glorious!

And sought to inhale their fragrance at a time that knoweth neither beginning nor end.

Glorified be my Lord, the All-Glorious!

She found not in them that which she did desire, and this, verily, is but one of His wondrous tales.

Glorified be my Lord, the All-Glorious!

She then cried aloud, wailed and repaired to her own station within her most lofty mansion,

Glorified be my Lord, the All-Glorious!

And then gave utterance to one mystic word, whispered privily by her honeyed tongue,

Glorified be my Lord, the All-Glorious!

And raised the call amidst the Celestial Concourse and the immortal maids of heaven:

Glorified be my Lord, the All-Glorious!

"By the Lord! I found not from these idle claimants the breeze of Faithfulness!

Glorified be my Lord, the All-Glorious!

"By the Lord! The Youth hath remained lone and forlorn in the land of exile in the hands of the ungodly."

Glorified be my Lord, the All-Glorious!

She then uttered within herself such a cry that the Celestial Concourse did shriek and tremble,

Glorified be my Lord, the All-Glorious!

And she fell upon the dust and gave up the spirit. It seemeth she was called and hearkened unto Him that summoned her unto the Realm on High.

Glorified be my Lord, the All-Glorious!

Glorified be He that created her out of the essence of love in the midmost heart of His exalted paradise!

Glorified be my Lord, the All-Glorious!

Thereupon the maids of heaven hastened forth from their chambers, upon whose countenances the eye of no dweller in the highest paradise had ever gazed.

Glorified be our Lord, the Most High!

They all gathered around her, and lo! they found her body fallen upon the dust;

Glorified be our Lord, the Most High!

And as they beheld her state and comprehended a word of the tale told by the Youth, they bared their heads, rent their garments asunder, beat upon their faces, forgot their joy, shed tears and smote with their hands upon their cheeks, and this is verily one of the mysterious grievous afflictions—

Glorified be our Lord, the Most High!

—*Bahá'u'lláh*

Tablets of Visitation

This Tablet is read at the Shrines of Bahá'u'lláh and the Báb. It is also frequently used in commemorating Their anniversaries (births and ascensions).*

* *Bahá'í Prayers,* p. 332

Tablet of Visitation

The praise which hath dawned from Thy most august Self, and the glory which hath shone forth from Thy most effulgent Beauty, rest upon Thee, O Thou Who art the Manifestation of Grandeur, and the King of Eternity, and the Lord of all who are in heaven and on earth! I testify that through Thee the sovereignty of God and His dominion, and the majesty of God and His grandeur, were revealed, and the Daystars of ancient splendor have shed their radiance in the heaven of Thine irrevocable decree, and the Beauty of the Unseen hath shone forth above the horizon of creation. I testify, moreover, that with but a movement of Thy Pen Thine injunction "Be Thou" hath been enforced, and God's hidden Secret hath been divulged, and all created things have been called into being, and all the Revelations have been sent down.

I bear witness, moreover, that through Thy beauty the beauty of the Adored One hath been unveiled, and through Thy face the face of the Desired One hath shone forth, and that through a word from Thee Thou hast decided between all created things, causing them who are devoted to Thee to ascend unto the summit of glory, and the infidels to fall into the lowest abyss.

I bear witness that he who hath known Thee hath known God, and he who hath attained unto Thy presence hath attained unto the presence of God. Great, therefore, is the blessedness of him who hath believed in Thee, and in Thy signs, and hath humbled himself before Thy sovereignty, and hath been honored with meeting Thee, and hath attained the good pleasure of Thy will, and circled around Thee, and stood before Thy throne. Woe betide him that hath transgressed against Thee, and hath denied Thee, and repudiated Thy signs, and gainsaid Thy sovereignty, and risen up against Thee, and waxed proud before Thy face, and hath disputed Thy testimonies, and fled from Thy rule and Thy dominion, and been numbered with the infidels whose names have been inscribed by the fingers of Thy behest upon Thy holy Tablets.

Waft, then, unto me, O my God and my Beloved, from the right hand of Thy mercy and Thy loving-kindness, the holy breaths of Thy favors, that they may draw me away from myself and from the world unto the courts of Thy nearness and Thy presence. Potent art Thou to do what pleaseth Thee. Thou, truly, hast been supreme over all things.

The remembrance of God and His praise, and the glory of God and His splendor, rest upon

Thee, O Thou Who art His Beauty! I bear witness that the eye of creation hath never gazed upon one wronged like Thee. Thou wast immersed all the days of Thy life beneath an ocean of tribulations. At one time Thou wast in chains and fetters; at another Thou wast threatened by the sword of Thine enemies. Yet, despite all this, Thou didst enjoin upon all men to observe what had been prescribed unto Thee by Him Who is the All-Knowing, the All-Wise.

May my spirit be a sacrifice to the wrongs Thou didst suffer, and my soul be a ransom for the adversities Thou didst sustain. I beseech God, by Thee and by them whose faces have been illumined with the splendors of the light of Thy countenance, and who, for love of Thee, have observed all whereunto they were bidden, to remove the veils that have come in between Thee and Thy creatures, and to supply me with the good of this world and the world to come. Thou art, in truth, the Almighty, the Most Exalted, the All-Glorious, the Ever-Forgiving, the Most Compassionate.

Bless Thou, O Lord my God, the Divine Lote-Tree and its leaves, and its boughs, and its branches, and its stems, and its offshoots, as long as Thy most excellent titles will endure and Thy most august attributes will last. Protect it, then, from the mischief of the aggressor and the hosts of tyranny. Thou art, in truth, the Almighty, the Most Powerful. Bless Thou, also, O Lord my God, Thy servants and Thy handmaidens who have attained unto Thee. Thou, truly, art the All-Bountiful, Whose grace is infinite. No God is there save Thee, the Ever-Forgiving, the Most Generous.

—*Bahá'u'lláh*

Tablet of Visitation

This prayer, which is different from the previous Tablet of Visitation, was revealed by 'Abdu'l-Bahá and is read at His Shrine. It is also used in private prayer.*

Whoso reciteth this prayer with lowliness and fervor will bring gladness and joy to the heart of this Servant; it will be even as meeting Him face to face.

He is the All-Glorious!

O God, my God! Lowly and tearful, I raise my suppliant hands to Thee and cover my face in the dust of that Threshold of Thine, exalted above the knowledge of the learned, and the praise of all that glorify Thee. Graciously look upon Thy servant, humble and lowly at Thy door, with the glances of the eye of Thy mercy, and immerse him in the Ocean of Thine eternal grace.

Lord! He is a poor and lowly servant of Thine, enthralled and imploring Thee, captive in Thy hand, praying fervently to Thee, trusting in Thee, in tears before Thy face, calling to Thee and beseeching Thee, saying:

---

* *Bahá'í Prayers,* p. 328.

O Lord, my God! Give me Thy grace to serve Thy loved ones, strengthen me in my servitude to Thee, illumine my brow with the light of adoration in Thy court of holiness, and of prayer to Thy kingdom of grandeur. Help me to be selfless at the heavenly entrance of Thy gate, and aid me to be detached from all things within Thy holy precincts. Lord! Give me to drink from the chalice of selflessness; with its robe clothe me, and in its ocean immerse me. Make me as dust in the pathway of Thy loved ones, and grant that I may offer up my soul for the earth ennobled by the footsteps of Thy chosen ones in Thy path, O Lord of Glory in the Highest.

With this prayer doth Thy servant call Thee, at dawntide and in the night-season. Fulfill his heart's desire, O Lord! Illumine his heart, gladden his bosom, kindle his light, that he may serve Thy Cause and Thy servants.

Thou art the Bestower, the Pitiful, the Most Bountiful, the Gracious, the Merciful, the Compassionate.

—*'Abdu'l-Bahá*

Tablet of Carmel

This tablet was revealed by Bahá'u'lláh on Mount Carmel, in Haifa, Israel, probably on His fourth visit to that spot in 1891. The tablet contains significant allusions to the establishment of the Bahá'í World Center and is stated by Shoghi Effendi to be its charter. The Bahá'í World Center is located on Mount Carmel in Haifa, Israel.*

* Momen, *A Basic Bahá'í Dictionary,* pp. 218–19.

Lawḥ-i-Karmil (Tablet of Carmel)

All glory be to this Day, the Day in which the fragrances of mercy have been wafted over all created things, a Day so blest that past ages and centuries can never hope to rival it, a Day in which the countenance of the Ancient of Days hath turned towards His holy seat. Thereupon the voices of all created things, and beyond them those of the Concourse on High, were heard calling aloud: 'Haste thee, O Carmel, for lo, the light of the countenance of God, the Ruler of the Kingdom of Names and Fashioner of the heavens, hath been lifted upon thee.'

Seized with transports of joy, and raising high her voice, she thus exclaimed: 'May my life be a sacrifice to Thee, inasmuch as Thou hast fixed Thy gaze upon me, hast bestowed upon me Thy bounty, and hast directed towards me Thy steps. Separation from Thee, O Thou Source of everlasting life, hath well nigh consumed me, and my remoteness from Thy presence hath burned away my soul. All praise be to Thee for having enabled me to hearken to Thy call, for having honoured me with Thy footsteps, and for having quickened my soul through the vitalizing fragrance of Thy Day and the shrilling voice of Thy Pen, a voice Thou didst ordain as Thy trumpet-call amidst

Thy people. And when the hour at which Thy resistless Faith was to be made manifest did strike, Thou didst breathe a breath of Thy spirit into Thy Pen, and lo, the entire creation shook to its very foundations, unveiling to mankind such mysteries as lay hidden within the treasuries of Him Who is the Possessor of all created things.'

No sooner had her voice reached that most exalted Spot than We made reply: 'Render thanks unto thy Lord, O Carmel. The fire of thy separation from Me was fast consuming thee, when the ocean of My presence surged before thy face, cheering thine eyes and those of all creation, and filling with delight all things visible and invisible. Rejoice, for God hath in this Day established upon thee His throne, hath made thee the dawning-place of His signs and the dayspring of the evidences of His Revelation. Well is it with him that circleth around thee, that proclaimeth the revelation of thy glory, and recounteth that which the bounty of the Lord thy God hath showered upon thee. Seize thou the Chalice of Immortality in the name of thy Lord, the All-Glorious, and give thanks unto Him, inasmuch as He, in token of His mercy unto thee, hath turned thy sorrow into gladness, and transmuted thy grief into blissful joy. He, verily, loveth the spot which hath been made the seat of His throne, which His footsteps have trodden, which hath been honoured by His presence, from which He raised His call, and upon which He shed His tear 'Call out to Zion, O Carmel, and announce the joyful tidings: He that was hidden from mortal eyes is come! His all-conquering sovereignty is manifest; His all-encompassing splendour is revealed. Beware lest thou hesitate or halt. Hasten forth and circumambulate the City of God that hath descended from heaven, the celestial Kaaba round which have circled in adoration the favoured of God, the pure in heart, and the company of the most exalted angels. Oh, how I long to announce unto every spot on the surface of the earth, and to carry to each one of its cities, the glad-tidings of this Revelation—a Revelation to which the heart of Sinai hath been attracted, and in whose name the Burning Bush is calling: "Unto God, the Lord of Lords, belong the kingdoms of earth and heaven." Verily this is the Day in which both land and sea rejoice at this announcement, the Day for which have been laid up those things which God, through a bounty beyond the ken of mortal mind or heart, hath destined for revelation. Ere long will God sail His Ark upon thee, and will manifest the people of Bahá who have been mentioned in the Book of Names.'

Sanctified be the Lord of all mankind, at the mention of Whose name all the atoms of the earth have been made to vibrate, and the Tongue of Grandeur hath been moved to disclose that which had been wrapt in His knowledge and lay concealed within the treasury of His might. He, verily, through the potency of His name, the Mighty, the All-Powerful, the Most High, is the ruler of all that is in the heavens and all that is on earth.

Tablet of Wisdom

Bahá'u'lláh addressed this tablet to a Bahá'í named Áqá Muḥammad-i-Qá'iní, a distinguished believer who was also known as Nabíl-i-Akbar (see *Memorials of the Faithful,* pages 1–5). Sometime between 1873 and 1874, Bahá'u'lláh revealed the tablet during Nabíl-i-Akbar's pilgrimage to the city of 'Akká, in present-day Israel, where Bahá'u'lláh was staying. Some of the themes of this tablet include the influence of the Word of God, the cause and origin of creation, and the mysterious workings of nature.*

---

* Taherzadeh, *The Revelation of Bahá'u'lláh,* 4:33.

Lawḥ-i-Hikmat (Tablet of Wisdom)

This is an Epistle which the All-Merciful hath sent down from the Kingdom of Utterance. It is truly a breath of life unto those who dwell in the realm of creation. Glorified be the Lord of all worlds! In this Epistle mention is made of him who magnifieth the Name of God, his Lord, and who is named Nabíl in a weighty Tablet.

O Muḥammad! Hearken unto the Voice proceeding out of the Realm of Glory, calling aloud from the celestial Tree which hath risen above the land of Za'farán*: Verily, no God is there but Me, the Omniscient, the Wise. Be thou as the breezes of the All-Merciful for the trees of the realm of existence and foster their growth through the potency of the Name of thy Lord, the Just, the All-Informed. We desire to acquaint thee with that which will serve as a reminder unto the people, that they may put away the things current amongst them and set their faces towards God, the Lord of the sincere.

---

* In a Tablet Bahá'u'lláh states, "The Holy Tree [Sadrat] is, in a sense, the Manifestation of the One True God, exalted be He. The Blessed Tree in the land of Za'farán referreth to the land which is flourishing, blessed, holy and all-perfumed, where that Tree hath been planted."

We exhort mankind in these days when the countenance of Justice is soiled with dust, when the flames of unbelief are burning high and the robe of wisdom rent asunder, when tranquillity and faithfulness have ebbed away and trials and tribulations have waxed severe, when covenants are broken and ties are severed, when no man knoweth how to discern light and darkness or to distinguish guidance from error.

O peoples of the world! Forsake all evil, hold fast that which is good. Strive to be shining examples unto all mankind, and true reminders of the virtues of God amidst men. He that riseth to serve My Cause should manifest My wisdom, and bend every effort to banish ignorance from the earth. Be united in counsel, be one in thought. Let each morn be better than its eve and each morrow richer than its yesterday. Man's merit lieth in service and virtue and not in the pageantry of wealth and riches. Take heed that your words be purged from idle fancies and worldly desires and your deeds be cleansed from craftiness and suspicion. Dissipate not the wealth of your precious lives in the pursuit of evil and corrupt affection, nor let your endeavours be spent in promoting your personal interest. Be generous in your days of plenty, and be patient in the hour of loss. Adversity is followed by success and rejoicings follow woe. Guard against idleness and sloth, and cling unto that which profiteth mankind, whether young or old, whether high or low. Beware lest ye sow tares of dissension among men or plant thorns of doubt in pure and radiant hearts.

O ye beloved of the Lord! Commit not that which defileth the limpid stream of love or destroyeth the sweet fragrance of friendship. By the righteousness of the Lord! Ye were created to show love one to another and not perversity and rancour. Take pride not in love for yourselves but in love for your fellow-creatures. Glory not in love for your country, but in love for all mankind. Let your eye be chaste, your hand faithful, your tongue truthful and your heart enlightened. Abase not the station of the learned in Bahá and belittle not the rank of such rulers as administer justice amidst you. Set your reliance on the army of justice, put on the armour of wisdom, let your adorning be forgiveness and mercy and that which cheereth the hearts of the well-favoured of God.

By My life! Thy grievances have plunged Me into sorrow. Regard not the children of the world and all their doings but fix thy gaze upon God and His never-ending dominion. Verily, He calleth to thy remembrance that which is the source of delight for all mankind. Drink thou the life-giving water of blissful joy from the chalice of utterance proffered by the Fountainhead of divine Revelation—He Who hath made mention of thee in this mighty stronghold. Endeavour to the utmost of thy powers to establish the word of truth with eloquence and wisdom and to dispel falsehood from the face of the earth. Thus directeth thee the Dayspring of divine knowledge from this luminous horizon.

O thou who speakest in My Name! Consider the people and the things they have wrought in My days. We revealed unto one of the rulers that which overpowereth all the dwellers of the earth, and requested him to bring Us face to face with the learned men of this age, that We might set forth for him the testimony of God, His proofs, His glory and His majesty; and naught did We intend thereby but the highest good. However, he committed that which hath caused the inmates of the cities of justice and equity to lament. Thus hath judgement been given between Me and him. Verily thy Lord is the Ordainer, the All-Informed. In such circumstances as thou seest, how can the Celestial Bird soar into the atmosphere of divine mysteries when its wings have been battered with the stones of idle fancy and bitter hatred, and it is cast into a prison built of unyielding stone? By the righteousness of God! The people have perpetrated a grievous injustice.

As regards thine assertions about the beginning of creation, this is a matter on which conceptions vary by reason of the divergences in men's thoughts and opinions. Wert thou to assert that it hath ever existed and shall continue to exist, it would be true; or wert thou to affirm the same concept as is mentioned in the sacred Scriptures, no doubt would there be about it, for it hath been revealed by God, the Lord of the worlds. Indeed He was a hidden treasure. This is a station that can never be described nor even alluded to. And in the station of 'I did wish to make Myself known', God was, and His creation had ever existed beneath His shelter from the beginning that hath no beginning, apart from its being preceded by a Firstness which cannot be regarded as firstness and originated by a Cause inscrutable even unto all men of learning.

That which hath been in existence had existed before, but not in the form thou seest today. The world of existence came into being through the heat generated from the interaction between the active force and that which is its recipient. These two are the same, yet they are different. Thus doth the Great Announcement inform thee about this glorious structure. Such as communicate the generating influence and such as receive its impact are indeed created through the irresistible Word of God which is the Cause of the entire creation, while all else besides His Word are but the creatures and the effects thereof. Verily thy Lord is the Expounder, the All-Wise.

Know thou, moreover, that the Word of God—exalted be His glory—is higher and far superior to that which the senses can perceive, for it is sanctified from any property or substance. It transcendeth the limitations of known elements and is exalted above all the essential and recognized substances. It became manifest without any syllable or sound and is none but the Command of God which pervadeth all created things. It hath never been withheld from the world of being. It is God's all-pervasive grace, from which all grace doth emanate. It is an entity far removed above all that hath been and shall be.

We are loath to enlarge on this subject, inasmuch as the unbelievers have inclined their ears towards Us in order to hear that which might enable them to cavil against God, the Help in Peril, the Self-Subsisting. And since they are unable to attain to mysteries of knowledge and wisdom from what hath been unravelled by the Source of divine splendour, they rise in protest and burst into clamour. But it is true to say that they object to that which they comprehend, not to the expositions given by the Expounder, nor the truths imparted by the One true God, the Knower of things unseen. Their objections, one and all, turn upon themselves, and I swear by thy life that they are devoid of understanding.

Every thing must needs have an origin and every building a builder. Verily, the Word of God is the Cause which hath preceded the contingent world—a world which is adorned with the splendours of the Ancient of Days, yet is being renewed and regenerated at all times. Immeasurably exalted is the God of Wisdom Who hath raised this sublime structure.

Look at the world and ponder a while upon it. It unveileth the book of its own self before thine eyes and revealeth that which the Pen of thy Lord, the Fashioner, the All-Informed, hath inscribed therein. It will acquaint thee with that which is within it and upon it and will give thee such clear explanations as to make thee independent of every eloquent expounder.

Say: Nature in its essence is the embodiment of My Name, the Maker, the Creator. Its manifestations are diversified by varying causes, and in this diversity there are signs for men of discernment. Nature is God's Will and is its expression in and through the contingent world. It is a dispensation of Providence ordained by the Ordainer, the All-Wise. Were anyone to affirm that it is the Will of God as manifested in the world of being, no one should question this assertion. It is endowed with a power whose reality men of learning fail to grasp. Indeed a man of insight can perceive naught therein save the effulgent splendour of Our Name, the Creator. Say: This is an existence which knoweth no decay, and Nature itself is lost in bewilderment before its revelations, its compelling evidences and its effulgent glory which have encompassed the universe.

It ill beseemeth thee to turn thy gaze unto former or more recent times. Make thou mention of this Day and magnify that which hath appeared therein. It will in truth suffice all mankind. Indeed expositions and discourses in explanation of such things cause the spirits to be chilled. It behoveth thee to speak forth in such wise as to set the hearts of true believers ablaze and cause their bodies to soar.

Whoso firmly believeth today in the rebirth of man and is fully conscious that God, the Most Exalted, wieldeth supreme ascendancy and absolute authority over this new creation, verily such a man is reckoned with them that are endued with insight in this most great Revelation. Unto this beareth witness every discerning believer.

Walk thou high above the world of being through the power of the Most Great Name, that thou mayest become aware of the immemorial mysteries and be acquainted with that wherewith no one is acquainted. Verily, thy Lord is the Helper, the All-Knowing, the All-Informed. Be thou as a throbbing artery, pulsating in the body of the entire creation, that through the heat generated by this motion there may appear that which will quicken the hearts of those who hesitate.

At the time when We were hidden behind countless veils of light thou didst commune with Me and didst witness the luminaries of the heaven of My wisdom and the billows of the ocean of Mine utterance. Verily thy Lord is the Truthful, the Faithful. Great indeed is the blessedness of him who hath attained the liberal effusions of this ocean in the days of his Lord, the Most Bountiful, the All-Wise.

During Our sojourn in 'Iráq when We were at the house of one named Majíd, We set forth clearly for thee the mysteries of creation and the origin, the culmination and the cause thereof. However since Our departure We have limited Ourself to this affirmation: 'Verily, no God is there but Me, the Ever-Forgiving, the Bountiful.'

Teach thou the Cause of God with an utterance which will cause the bushes to be enkindled, and the call 'Verily, there is no God but Me, the Almighty, the Unconstrained' to be raised therefrom. Say: Human utterance is an essence which aspireth to exert its influence and needeth moderation. As to its influence, this is conditional upon refinement which in turn is dependent upon hearts which are detached and pure. As to its moderation, this hath to be combined with tact and wisdom as prescribed in the Holy Scriptures and Tablets. Meditate upon that which hath streamed forth from the heaven of the Will of thy Lord, He Who is the Source of all grace, that thou mayest grasp the intended meaning which is enshrined in the sacred depths of the Holy Writings.

Those who have rejected God and firmly cling to Nature as it is in itself are, verily, bereft of knowledge and wisdom. They are truly of them that are far astray. They have failed to attain the lofty summit and have fallen short of the ultimate purpose; therefore their eyes were shut and their thoughts differed, while the leaders among them have believed in God and in His invincible sovereignty. Unto this beareth witness thy Lord, the Help in Peril, the Self-Subsisting.

When the eyes of the people of the East were captivated by the arts and wonders of the West, they roved distraught in the wilderness of material causes, oblivious of the One Who is the Causer of Causes, and the Sustainer thereof, while such men as were the source and the wellspring of Wisdom never denied the moving Impulse behind these causes, nor the Creator or the Origin thereof. Thy Lord knoweth, yet most of the people know not.

Now We have, for the sake of God, the Lord of Names, set Ourself the task of mentioning in this Tablet some accounts of the sages,* that the eyes of the people may be opened thereby and that they may become fully assured that He is in truth the Maker, the Omnipotent, the Creator, the Originator, the All-Knowing, the All-Wise.

Although it is recognized that the contemporary men of learning are highly qualified in philosophy, arts and crafts, yet were anyone to observe with a discriminating eye he would readily comprehend that most of this knowledge hath been acquired from the sages of the past, for it is they who have laid the foundation of philosophy, reared its structure and reinforced its pillars. Thus doth thy Lord, the Ancient of Days, inform thee. The sages aforetime acquired their knowledge from the Prophets, inasmuch as the latter were the Exponents of divine philosophy and the Revealers of heavenly mysteries. Men quaffed the crystal, living waters of Their utterance, while others satisfied themselves with the dregs. Everyone receiveth a portion according to his measure. Verily He is the Equitable, the Wise.

---

* In many of the passages that follow concerning the Greek philosophers, Bahá'u'lláh quotes verbatim from the works of such Muslim historians as Abu'l-Fatḥ-i-Sháhristání (1076–1153 A.D.) and Imádu'd-Dín Abu'l-Fidá (1273–1331 A.D.).

Empedocles, who distinguished himself in philosophy, was a contemporary of David, while Pythagoras lived in the days of Solomon, son of David, and acquired Wisdom from the treasury of prophethood. It is he who claimed to have heard the whispering sound of the heavens and to have attained the station of the angels. In truth thy Lord will clearly set forth all things, if He pleaseth. Verily, He is the Wise, the All-Pervading.

The essence and the fundamentals of philosophy have emanated from the Prophets. That the people differ concerning the inner meanings and mysteries thereof is to be attributed to the divergence of their views and minds. We would fain recount to thee the following: One of the Prophets once was communicating to his people that with which the Omnipotent Lord had inspired Him. Truly, thy Lord is the Inspirer, the Gracious, the Exalted. When the fountain of wisdom and eloquence gushed forth from the wellspring of His utterance and the wine of divine knowledge inebriated those who had sought His threshold, He exclaimed: 'Lo! All are filled with the Spirit.' From among the people there was he who held fast unto this statement and, actuated by his own fancies, conceived the idea that the spirit literally penetrateth or entereth into the body, and through lengthy expositions he advanced proofs to vindicate this concept; and groups of people followed in his footsteps. To mention their names at this point, or to give thee a detailed account thereof, would lead to prolixity, and would depart from the main theme. Verily, thy Lord is the All-Wise, the All-Knowing. There was also he who partook of the choice wine whose seal had been removed by the Key of the Tongue of Him Who is the Revealer of the Verses of thy Lord, the Gracious, the Most Generous.

Verily, the philosophers have not denied the Ancient of Days. Most of them passed away deploring their failure to fathom His mystery, even as some of them have testified. Verily, thy Lord is the Adviser, the All-Informed.

Consider Hippocrates, the physician. He was one of the eminent philosophers who believed in God and acknowledged His sovereignty. After him came Socrates who was indeed wise, accomplished and righteous. He practised self-denial, repressed his appetites for selfish desires and turned away from material pleasures. He withdrew to the mountains where he dwelt in a cave. He dissuaded men from worshipping idols and taught them the way of God, the Lord of Mercy, until the ignorant rose up against him. They arrested him and put him to death in prison. Thus relateth to thee this swift-moving Pen. What a penetrating vision into philosophy this eminent man had! He is the most distinguished of all philosophers and was highly versed in wisdom. We testify that he is one of the heroes in this field and an outstanding champion dedicated unto it. He had a profound knowledge of such sciences as were current amongst men as well as of those which were veiled from their minds. Methinks he drank one draught when the Most Great Ocean overflowed with gleaming and life-giving waters. He it is who perceived a unique, a tempered, and a pervasive nature in things, bearing the closest likeness to the human spirit, and he discovered this nature to be distinct from the substance of things in their refined form. He hath a special pronouncement on this weighty theme. Wert thou to ask from the worldly wise of this generation about this exposition, thou wouldst witness their incapacity to grasp it. Verily, thy Lord speaketh the truth but most people comprehend not.

After Socrates came the divine Plato who was a pupil of the former and occupied the chair of philosophy as his successor. He acknowledged his belief in God and in His signs which pervade all that hath been and shall be. Then came Aristotle, the well-known man of knowledge. He it is who discovered the power of gaseous matter. These men who stand out as leaders of the people and are pre-eminent among them, one and all acknowledged their belief in the immortal Being Who holdeth in His grasp the reins of all sciences.

I will also mention for thee the invocation voiced by Bálinus who was familiar with the theories put forward by the Father of Philosophy regarding the mysteries of creation as given in his chrysolite tablets, that everyone may be fully assured of the things We have elucidated for thee in this manifest Tablet, which, if pressed with the hand of fairness and knowledge, will yield the spirit of life for the quickening of all created things. Great is the blessedness of him who swimmeth in this ocean and celebrateth the praise of his Lord, the Gracious, the Best-Beloved. Indeed the breezes of divine revelation are diffused from the verses of thy Lord in such wise that no one can dispute its truth, except those who are bereft of hearing, of vision, of understanding and of every human faculty. Verily thy Lord beareth witness unto this, yet the people understand not.

This man hath said: 'I am Bálinus, the wise one, the performer of wonders, the producer of talismans.' He surpassed everyone else in the diffusion of arts and sciences and soared unto the loftiest heights of humility and supplication. Give ear unto that which he hath said, entreating the All-Possessing, the Most Exalted: 'I stand in the presence of my Lord, extolling His gifts and bounties and praising Him with that wherewith He praiseth His Own Self, that I may become a source of blessing and guidance unto such men as acknowledge my words.' And further he saith: 'O Lord! Thou art God and no God is there but Thee. Thou art the Creator and no creator is there except Thee. Assist me by Thy grace and strengthen me. My heart is seized with alarm, my limbs tremble, I have lost my reason and my mind hath failed me. Bestow upon me strength and enable my tongue to speak forth with wisdom.' And still further he saith: 'Thou art in truth the Knowing, the Wise, the Powerful, the Compassionate.' It was this man of wisdom who became informed of the mysteries of creation and discerned the subtleties which lie enshrined in the Hermetic writings.*

---

* In one of His Tablets Bahá'u'lláh wrote: 'The first person who devoted himself to philosophy was Ídrís. Thus was he named. Some called him also Hermes. In every tongue he hath a special name. He it is who hath set forth in every branch of philosophy thorough and convincing statements. After him Bálinus derived his knowledge and sciences from the Hermetic Tablets and most of the philosophers who followed him made their philosophical and scientific discoveries from his words and statements. . . .' In the Qur'án, Súra 19, verses 57 and 58, is written: 'And commemorate Ídrís in the Book; for he was a man of truth, a Prophet; And we uplifted him to a place on high.'

We have no wish to mention anything further but We shall utter that which the Spirit hath instilled into My heart. In truth there is no God but Him, the Knowing, the Mighty, the Help in Peril, the Most Excellent, the All-Praised. By My life! In this Day the celestial Tree is loath to proclaim aught else to the world but this affirmation: 'Verily, there is none other God but Me, the Peerless, the All-Informed.'

Had it not been for the love I cherish for thee, I would not have uttered a single word of what hath been mentioned. Appreciate the value of this station and preserve it as thou wouldst thine eye and be of them that are truly thankful.

Thou knowest full well that We perused not the books which men possess and We acquired not the learning current amongst them, and yet whenever We desire to quote the sayings of the learned and of the wise,* presently there will appear before the face of thy Lord in the form of a tablet all that which hath appeared in the world and is revealed in the Holy Books and Scriptures. Thus do We

* In many of the passages that follow concerning the Greek philosophers, Bahá'u'lláh quotes verbatim from the works of such Muslim historians as Abu'l-Fatḥ-i-Sháhristání (1076–1153 A.D.) and Imádu'd-Dín Abu'l-Fidá (1273–1331 A.D.).

set down in writing that which the eye perceiveth. Verily His knowledge encompasseth the earth and the heavens.

This is a Tablet wherein the Pen of the Unseen hath inscribed the knowledge of all that hath been and shall be—a knowledge that none other but My wondrous Tongue can interpret. Indeed My heart as it is in itself hath been purged by God from the concepts of the learned and is sanctified from the utterances of the wise. In truth naught doth it mirror forth but the revelations of God. Unto this beareth witness the Tongue of Grandeur in this perspicuous Book.

Say, O people of the earth! Beware lest any reference to wisdom debar you from its Source or withhold you from the Dawning-Place thereof. Fix your hearts upon your Lord, the Educator, the All-Wise.

For every land We have prescribed a portion, for every occasion an allotted share, for every pronouncement an appointed time and for every situation an apt remark. Consider Greece. We made it a Seat of Wisdom for a prolonged period. However, when the appointed hour struck, its throne was subverted, its tongue ceased to speak, its light grew dim and its banner was hauled down. Thus do We bestow and withdraw. Verily thy Lord is He Who giveth and divesteth, the Mighty, the Powerful.

In every land We have set up a luminary of knowledge, and when the time foreordained is at hand, it will shine resplendent above its horizon, as decreed by God, the All-Knowing, the All-Wise. If it be Our Will We are fully capable of describing for thee whatever existeth in every land or hath come to pass therein. Indeed the knowledge of thy Lord pervadeth the heavens and the earth.

Know thou, moreover, that the people aforetime have produced things which the contemporary men of knowledge have been unable to produce. We recall unto thee Murtús who was one of the learned. He invented an apparatus which transmitted sound over a distance of sixty miles. Others besides him have also discovered things which no one in this age hath beheld. Verily thy Lord revealeth in every epoch whatsoever He pleaseth as a token of wisdom on His part. He is in truth the supreme Ordainer, the All-Wise.

A true philosopher would never deny God nor His evidences, rather would he acknowledge His glory and overpowering majesty which overshadow all created things. Verily We love those men of knowledge who have brought to light such things as promote the best interests of humanity, and We aided them through the potency of Our behest, for well are We able to achieve Our purpose.

Beware, O My loved ones, lest ye despise the merits of My learned servants whom God hath graciously chosen to be the exponents of His Name 'the Fashioner' amidst mankind. Exert your utmost endeavour that ye may develop such crafts and undertakings that everyone, whether young or old, may benefit therefrom. We are quit of those ignorant ones who fondly imagine that Wisdom is to give vent to one's idle imaginings and to repudiate God, the Lord of all men; even as We hear some of the heedless voicing such assertions today.

Say: The beginning of Wisdom and the origin thereof is to acknowledge whatsoever God hath clearly set forth, for through its potency the foundation of statesmanship, which is a shield for the preservation of the body of mankind, hath been firmly established. Ponder a while that ye may perceive what My most exalted Pen hath proclaimed in this wondrous Tablet. Say, every matter related to state affairs which ye raise for discussion falls under the shadow of one of the words sent down from the heaven of His glorious and exalted utterance. Thus have We recounted unto thee that which will exhilarate thy heart, will bring solace to thine eyes and will enable thee to arise for the promotion of His Cause amidst all peoples.

O My Nabíl! Let nothing grieve thee, rather rejoice with exceeding gladness inasmuch as I have mentioned thy name, have turned My heart and My face towards thee and have conversed with thee through this irrefutable and weighty exposition.

Ponder in thy heart upon the tribulations I have sustained, the imprisonment and the captivity I have endured, the sufferings that have befallen Me and the accusations that the people have levelled against Me. Behold, they are truly wrapped in a grievous veil.

When the discourse reached this stage, the dawn of divine mysteries appeared and the light of utterance was quenched. May His glory rest upon the people of wisdom as bidden by One Who is the Almighty, the All-Praised.

Say: Magnified be Thy Name, O Lord my God! I beseech Thee by Thy Name through which the splendour of the light of wisdom shone resplendent when the heavens of divine utterance were set in motion amidst mankind, to graciously aid me by Thy heavenly confirmations and enable me to extol Thy Name amongst Thy servants.

O Lord! Unto Thee have I turned my face, detached from all save Thee and holding fast to the hem of the robe of Thy manifold blessings. Unloose my tongue therefore to proclaim that which will captivate the minds of men and will rejoice their souls and spirits. Strengthen me then in Thy Cause in such wise that I may not be hindered by the ascendancy of the oppressors among Thy creatures nor withheld by the onslaught of the disbelievers amidst those who dwell in Thy realm. Make me as a lamp shining throughout Thy lands that those in whose hearts the light of Thy knowledge gloweth and the yearning for Thy love lingereth may be guided by its radiance.

Verily, potent art Thou to do whatsoever Thou willest, and in Thy grasp Thou holdest the kingdom of creation. There is none other God but Thee, the Almighty, the All-Wise.

Words of Wisdom

Very little is known about the following tablet. For example, at the time of the publication of this book, it is not known when Bahá'u'lláh revealed this tablet, the circumstances surrounding its revelation, or whether it was addressed to a specific individual. "The source of all learning is the knowledge of God, exalted be His glory" is one of the quotations from this tablet used by Shoghi Effendi to adorn one of the doors of the House of Worship in Wilmette, Illinois.*

* Please see "Words of Wisdom: faculty notes by Rob Stockman, Iraj Ayman," at http://www.bahai-library.org/resources/tablets-notes/asl-kull-khayr/notes.html.

Asl-i-Kullu'l-Khayr (Words of Wisdom)
In the Name of God, the Exalted, the Most High

The source of all good is trust in God, submission unto His command, and contentment with His holy will and pleasure.

The essence of wisdom is the fear of God, the dread of His scourge and punishment, and the apprehension of His justice and decree.

The essence of religion is to testify unto that which the Lord hath revealed, and follow that which He hath ordained in His mighty Book.

The source of all glory is acceptance of whatsoever the Lord hath bestowed, and contentment with that which God hath ordained.

The essence of love is for man to turn his heart to the Beloved One, and sever himself from all else but Him, and desire naught save that which is the desire of his Lord.

True remembrance is to make mention of the Lord, the All-Praised, and forget aught else beside Him.

True reliance is for the servant to pursue his profession and calling in this world, to hold fast unto the Lord, to seek naught but His grace, inasmuch as in His Hands is the destiny of all His servants.

The essence of detachment is for man to turn his face towards the courts of the Lord, to enter

His Presence, behold His Countenance, and stand as witness before Him.

The essence of understanding is to testify to one's poverty, and submit to the Will of the Lord, the Sovereign, the Gracious, the All-Powerful.

The source of courage and power is the promotion of the Word of God, and steadfastness in His Love.

The essence of charity is for the servant to recount the blessings of his Lord, and to render thanks unto Him at all times and under all conditions.

The essence of faith is fewness of words and abundance of deeds; he whose words exceed his deeds, know verily his death is better than his life.

The essence of true safety is to observe silence, to look at the end of things and to renounce the world.

The beginning of magnanimity is when man expendeth his wealth on himself, on his family and on the poor among his brethren in his Faith.

The essence of wealth is love for Me; whoso loveth Me is the possessor of all things, and he that loveth Me not is indeed of the poor and needy. This is that which the Finger of Glory and Splendour hath revealed.

The source of all evil is for man to turn away from his Lord and set his heart on things ungodly.

The most burning fire is to question the signs of God, to dispute idly that which He hath revealed, to deny Him and carry one's self proudly before Him.

The source of all learning is the knowledge of God, exalted be His Glory, and this cannot be attained save through the knowledge of His Divine Manifestation.

The essence of abasement is to pass out from under the shadow of the Merciful and seek the shelter of the Evil One.

The source of error is to disbelieve in the One true God, rely upon aught else but Him, and flee from His Decree.

True loss is for him whose days have been spent in utter ignorance of his self.

The essence of all that We have revealed for thee is Justice, is for man to free himself from idle fancy and imitation, discern with the eye of oneness His glorious handiwork, and look into all things with a searching eye.

Thus have We instructed thee, manifested unto thee Words of Wisdom, that thou mayest be thankful unto the Lord, thy God, and glory therein amidst all peoples.

Notes

Aid and Assistance

1. *Prayers and Meditations,* pp. 101–2.
2. *Bahá'í Prayers,* pp. 23–24.
3. Ibid., pp. 22–23.
4. Ibid., pp. 24–25.

America

1. *Bahá'í Prayers,* p. 26.

Children

1. *Bahá'í Prayers,* pp. 32–33.
2. Ibid., p. 28.
3. Ibid., p. 28.
4. Ibid., pp. 33–34.
5. Ibid., pp. 28–29.
6. Ibid., pp. 30–31.

For the Departed

1. *Bahá'í Prayers,* pp. 37–38.
2. Ibid., p. 41.
3. Ibid., pp. 42–43.
4. Ibid., pp. 41–42.

Evening

1. *Bahá'í Prayers,* p. 59.
2. Ibid., p. 60.
3. Ibid., p. 61.

Family

1. *Bahá'í Prayers,* pp. 63–64.
2. Ibid., p. 64.
3. Ibid., p. 65.

Healing

1. *Bahá'í Prayers,* pp. 95–96.
2. Ibid., p. 96.
3. Ibid., pp. 96–97.
4. Ibid., pp. 97–99.
5. *Prayers and Meditations,* pp. 102–3.
6. *Bahá'í Prayers,* pp. 99–100.
7. Ibid., pp. 100–102.
8. Ibid., pp. 102–10.

Humanity

1. *Bahá'í Prayers,* pp. 111–12
2. Ibid., p. 112.
3. Ibid., pp. 112–13.
4. Ibid., pp. 113–15.

5. Ibid., pp. 115–16.

MARRIAGE

1. *Bahá'í Prayers,* pp. 117–18.
2. Ibid., pp. 118–20.
3. Ibid., p. 120.
4. Ibid., p. 121.

MORNING

1. *Bahá'í Prayers,* pp. 122–23.
2. Ibid., pp. 123–24.
3. Ibid., p. 124.
4. Ibid., pp. 124–26.

PROTECTION

1. *Bahá'í Prayers,* pp. 144–45.
2. Ibid., pp. 145–46.
3. Ibid., pp. 146–47.
4. Ibid., p. 147.
5. Ibid., pp. 148–49.
6. Ibid., pp. 149–50.
7. Ibid., pp. 150–51.
8. Ibid., pp. 151–53.
9. Ibid., pp. 153–54.
10. Ibid., p. 154.
11. Ibid., pp. 155–57.

TESTS AND DIFFICULTIES

1. *Bahá'í Prayers,* p. 220.
2. Ibid., pp. 220–22.
3. Ibid., pp. 222–23.

4. Ibid., pp. 223–24.
5. Ibid., pp. 224–25.
6. Ibid., p. 226.
7. Ibid., pp. 226–27.
8. Ibid., p. 227.
9. Ibid., pp. 227–28.

Unity

1. *Bahá'í Prayers,* p. 238.
2. Ibid., p. 239.

Women

1. *Bahá'í Prayers,* pp. 240–41.
2. Ibid., pp. 241–42.
3. Ibid., pp. 242–43.
4. Ibid., pp. 244–45.
5. Ibid., pp. 245–46.
6. Ibid., pp. 246–47.
7. Ibid., pp. 247–48.
8. Ibid., pp. 248–49.
9. Ibid., pp. 249–50.

Youth

1. *Bahá'í Prayers,* pp. 251–52.
2. Ibid., pp. 252–53.
3. Ibid., p. 253.
4. Ibid., p. 254.
5. Ibid., pp. 254–55.

Tablet of Aḥmad
Bahá'í Prayers, pp. 307–11.

Fire Tablet
Bahá'í Prayers, pp. 312–18.

Tablet of the Holy Mariner
Bahá'í Prayers, pp. 319–27.

Tablet of Visitation of Bahá'u'lláh and the Báb
Bahá'í Prayers, pp. 328–332.

Tablet of Visitation of 'Abdu'l-Bahá
Bahá'í Prayers, pp. 332–33.

Lawḥ-i-Karmil (Tablet of Carmel)
Tablets of Bahá'u'lláh, pp. 3–5.

Lawḥ-i-Hikmat (Tablet of Wisdom)
Tablets of Bahá'u'lláh, pp. 137–52.

Asl-i-Kullu'l-Khayr (Words of Wisdom)
Tablets of Bahá'u'lláh, pp. 155–57.

References

Works of Bahá'u'lláh

Gleanings from the Writings of Bahá'u'lláh. 1st pocket-size ed. Translated by Shoghi Effendi. Wilmette, IL: Bahá'í Publishing, 2005.

The Hidden Words. Translated by Shoghi Effendi. Wilmette, IL: Bahá'í Publishing, 2002.

Prayers and Meditations. Translated by Shoghi Effendi. 1st pocket-size ed. Wilmette, IL: Bahá'í Publishing Trust, 1987.

Tablets of Bahá'u'lláh revealed after the Kitáb-i-Aqdas. Compiled by the Research Department of the Universal House of Justice. Translated by Habib Taherzadeh et al. Wilmette, IL: Bahá'í Publishing Trust, 1988.

Works of 'Abdu'l-Bahá

O God, My God . . . Bahá'í Prayers and Tablets for Children and Youth. Wilmette, IL: Bahá'í Publishing Trust, 1984.

The Promulgation of Universal Peace: Talks Delivered by 'Abdu'l-Bahá during His Visit to the United States and Canada in 1912. Compiled by Howard MacNutt. Wilmette, IL: Bahá'í Publishing Trust, 2007.

Selections from the Writings of 'Abdu'l-Bahá. Compiled by the Research Department of the Universal House of Justice. Translated by a Committee at the Bahá'í World Center and Marzieh Gail. 1st pocket-size ed. Wilmette, IL: Bahá'í Publishing Trust, 1996.

Works of the Universal House of Justice

The Promise of World Peace: To the Peoples of the World. Wilmette, IL: Bahá'í Publishing Trust, 1985.

Compilations of Bahá'í Writings

Bahá'u'lláh, the Báb, and 'Abdu'l-Bahá. *Bahá'í Prayers: A Selection of Prayers Revealed by Bahá'u'lláh, the Báb, and 'Abdu'l-Bahá*. New ed. Wilmette, IL: Bahá'í Publishing Trust, 2002.

Other Works

Momen, Wendi. *A Basic Bahá'í Dictionary*. Oxford: George Ronald, 1989.

Taherzadeh, Adib. *The Revelation of Bahá'u'lláh: Baghdád, 1853–63*. Oxford: George Ronald, 1974.

———. *The Revelation of Bahá'u'lláh: Adrianople 1863–68*. Oxford: George Ronald, 1977.

———. *The Revelation of Bahá'u'lláh: 'Akká, The Early Years, 1868–77*. Oxford: George Ronald, 1983.

———. *The Revelation of Bahá'u'lláh: Mazra'ih & Bahjí, 1877–92*. Oxford: George Ronald, 1987.

Index of First Lines

"All glory be to this Day, the Day in which the fragrances of mercy . . ." 208
"Dispel my grief by Thy bounty and Thy generosity, O God, my God . . ." 138
"Glorified art Thou, O Lord my God! Every man of insight confesseth Thy sovereignty . . ." 137
"Glorified art Thou, O Lord my God! Thou art He the fire of Whose love . . ." 155
"Glory be to Thee, O God! Thou art the God Who hath existed . . ." 124
"Glory be to Thee, O Lord my God! Abase not him . . ." 58
"Glory be to Thee, O Lord my God! I beg of Thee by Thy name . . ." 80
"Glory be to Thee, O Lord my God! I implore Thee by Thy name . . ." 74
"Glory be to, O my God! My face hath been set towards Thy face, . . ." 154
"Glory be unto Thee, O my God! Verily, this Thy servant and this Thy maidservant . . ." 104
"Glory to Thee, O my God! But for the tribulations which are sustained in Thy path . . ." 135

"Glory to Thee, O my God! One of Thy handmaidens, who hath believed in Thee . . ." 161
"He is God! O peerless Lord! In Thine almighty wisdom Thou hast enjoined marriage . . ." 102
"He is the All-Glorious! O God, my God! Lowly and tearful, I raise my suppliant hands . . ." 204
"He is the Bestower, the Bounteous! Praise be to God, the Ancient . . ." 101
"He is the Gracious, the Well-Beloved! O Holy Mariner! Bid thine ark of eternity . . ." 190
"He is the Healer, the Sufficer, the Helper . . ." 84
"He is the King, the All-Knowing, the Wise! Lo, the Nightingale of Paradise singeth . . ." 178
"How can I choose to sleep, O God, my God . . ." 65
"I adjure Thee by Thy might, O my God! Let no harm beset me in times of tests . . ." 145
"I beg Thy forgiveness, O my God, and implore pardon . . ." 68
"I give praise to Thee, O my God, that Thou hast awakened me out of my sleep . . ." 112
"I have risen this morning by Thy grace, O my God, and left my home . . ." 111
"I have wakened in Thy shelter, O my God, and it becometh him . . ." 110
"In His Name, the Exalted, the All-Highest, the Most Sublime! . . ." 121
"In the Name of God, the Lord of overpowering majesty, the All-Compelling . . ." 125
"In the Name of God, the Most Ancient, the Most Great. Indeed the hearts . . ." 182
"Is there any Remover of difficulties save God? Say: Praised be God! . . ." 142

"Lauded and glorified art Thou, O my God! I entreat Thee . . ." 140
"Lauded be Thy name, O Lord my God! I entreat Thee by Thy Name . . ." 119
"Lord! Pitiful are we, grant us Thy favor . . ." 45
"Magnified be Thy name, O Lord my God! Behold Thou mine eye . . ." 157
"My God, Whom I worship and adore! I bear witness . . ." 92
"My Lord! My Lord! I praise Thee and I thank Thee for that whereby . . ." 165
"O God! Educate these children . . ." 51
"O God, my God! I beg of Thee by the ocean of Thy healing . . ." 72
"O God, my God! I have set out from my home, holding fast . . ." 120
"O God, my God! Shield Thy trusted servants from the evils of self and passion . . ." 127
"O God, my God! This Thy handmaid is calling upon Thee . . ." 70
"O God, O Thou Who hast cast Thy splendor over the luminous realities of men . . ." 97
"O God! Rear this little babe . . ." 53
"O Lord, I have turned my face unto Thy kingdom of oneness . . ." 66
"O Lord! In this Most Great Dispensation Thou dost accept . . ." 69
"O Lord! Make these children excellent plants . . ." 54
"O Lord! Make this youth radiant, and confer Thy bounty upon this poor creature . . ." 172
"O Lord! Thou art the Remover of every anguish and the Dispeller of every affliction . . ." 146

"O my God and my Master! I am Thy servant and the son of Thy servant . . ." 108
"O my God, my Master, the Goal of my desire! . . ." 64
"O my God! O my God! Unite the hearts of Thy servants . . ." 149
"O my God! O my God! Verily, I invoke Thee and supplicate before Thy threshold . . ." 150
"O my God! O my God! Verily, Thy servant, humble before the majesty . . ." 62
"O my God! O Thou forgiver of sins, bestower of gifts . . ." 60
"O my Lord, my Beloved, my Desire! Befriend me in my loneliness . . ." 164
"O my Lord, O my Lord! These two bright orbs are wedded in Thy love . . ." 105
"O my Lord! Thou knowest that the people are encircled with pain and calamities . . ." 128
"O Peerless Lord! Be Thou a shelter for this poor child . . ." 55
"Ordain for me, O my Lord, and for those who believe in Thee . . ." 123
"O Thou, at Whose dreadful majesty all things have trembled . . ." 159
"O Thou compassionate Lord, Thou Who art generous and able! We are servants . . ." 93
"O Thou forgiving Lord! Although some souls have spent the days of their lives . . ." 61
"O Thou kind and loving Providence! The east is astir and the west surgeth . . ." 129
"O Thou kind Lord! Bestow heavenly confirmation upon this daughter of the kingdom . . ." 171

"O Thou kind Lord! From the horizon of detachment Thou hast manifested souls that, . . ." 168
"O Thou kind Lord! Graciously bestow a pair of heavenly wings . . ." 170
"O Thou kind Lord! O Thou Who art generous and merciful! . . ." 94
"O Thou kind Lord! These lovely children . . ." 52
"O Thou kind Lord! This gathering is turning to Thee . . ." 48
"O Thou kind Lord! Thou hast created all humanity from the same stock . . ." 95
"O Thou kind Lord! We are servants of Thy Threshold . . ." 44
"O Thou Whose face is the object of the adoration of all that yearn after Thee, . . ." 153
"O Thou Whose tests are a healing medicine to such as are nigh unto Thee . . ." 134
"Praise and glory be to Thee, O Lord my God! This is a choice sapling . . ." 173
"Praise be to Thee, O Lord my God, my Master! Thou hearest the sighing . . ." 78
"Praise be to Thee, O Lord my God! Thou seest and knowest that I have called upon Thy servants . . ." 116
"Praised be Thou, O Lord my God! Graciously grant that this infant . . ." 50
"Praised be Thou, O Lord my God! I implore Thee, by Thy Most Great Name . . ." 76
"Praised be Thou, O Lord my God! This is Thy servant who hath quaffed . . ." 118
"Remove not, O Lord, the festal board that hath been spread in Thy name . . ." 46

"The praise which hath dawned from Thy most august Self, and the glory . . ." 200
"The source of all good is trust in God, submission unto His command . . ." 238
"This is an Epistle which the All-Merciful hath sent down from the Kingdom of Utterance . . ." 214
"Thou art He, O my God, through Whose names the sick are healed . . ." 82
"Thou beholdest, O my God, Thy servant who dwelleth in this prison-house . . ." 42
"Thou knowest full well, O my God, that tribulations have showered upon me . . ." 143
"Thou seest, O my God, how the wrongs committed by such of Thy creatures . . ." 163
"Thy name is my healing, O my God . . ." 73
"We will all, verily, abide by the Will of God . . ." 100

Bahá'í PUBLISHING

AND THE BAHÁ'Í FAITH

Bahá'í Publishing produces books based on the teachings of the Bahá'í Faith. Founded over 160 years ago, the Bahá'í Faith has spread to some 235 nations and territories and is now accepted by more than five million people. The word "Bahá'í" means "follower of Bahá'u'lláh." Bahá'u'lláh, the founder of the Bahá'í Faith, asserted that He is the Messenger of God for all of humanity in this day. The cornerstone of His teachings is the establishment of the spiritual unity of humankind, which will be achieved by personal transformation and the application of clearly identified spiritual principles. Bahá'ís also believe that there is but one religion and that all the Messengers of God—among them Abraham, Zoroaster, Moses, Krishna, Buddha, Jesus, and Muḥammad—have progressively revealed its nature. Together, the world's great religions are expressions of a single, unfolding divine plan. Human beings, not God's Messengers, are the source of religious divisions, prejudices, and hatreds.

The Bahá'í Faith is not a sect or denomination of another religion, nor is it a cult or a social movement. Rather, it is a globally recognized independent world religion founded on new books of scripture revealed by Bahá'u'lláh.

Bahá'í Publishing is an imprint of the National Spiritual Assembly of the Bahá'ís of the United States.

For more information about the Bahá'í Faith,
or to contact Bahá'ís near you,
visit http://www.bahai.us/
or call
1-800-22-UNITE

OTHER BOOKS AVAILABLE FROM BAHÁ'Í PUBLISHING

HERITAGE OF LIGHT
THE SPIRITUAL DESTINY OF AMERICA
Janet A. Khan
$17.00 US / $19.00 CAN
Trade Paper
ISBN 978-1-931847-73-5

An examination of a fascinating religious community and a penetrating look at the spiritual destiny of America.

Heritage of Light is an accessible description of the American Bahá'í community and a penetrating look at the spiritual destiny of America. This exploration traces the historical and spiritual connections that link the American Bahá'ís with the early Bahá'ís of Iran, who displayed an unparalleled staunchness of faith and heroism in the face of unspeakable brutal persecution and oppression. The author's examination of the writings of the Bahá'í Faith, along with extensive historical and archival records, demonstrates the unique role assigned to the American Bahá'ís and to the American nation as a whole in the development of a unified global society and the eventual inauguration of a world civilization.

UNDERSTANDING DEATH
THE MOST IMPORTANT EVENT
OF YOUR LIFE
John S. Hatcher
$18.00 US / $20.00 CAN
Trade Paper
ISBN 978-1-931847-72-8

A personal exploration of mortality and death, the inevitable journey of human life, and the acceptance of faith

Understanding Death: The Most Important Event of Your Life illustrates the need to prepare for this important moment, even though many ignore its inevitability. There is no escape from death and the grief that can consume one when faced by the loss of family and friends. The author's personal insight offers encouragement that death is not the end but the beginning of a new spiritual existence. Author John Hatcher surveys his own life, the decisions he has made over the years, and how those experiences have impacted him. He especially focuses on his discovery and exploration of the Bahá'í Faith and his eventual acceptance of Bahá'u'lláh's teachings. Accepting that death is not the end, that there is another journey, and that there is time to accept the inevitable and prepare for the life hereafter can bring peace and comfort to all.

MIND, HEART, & SPIRIT
EDUCATORS SPEAK
Heather Cardin
$18.00 US / $20.00 CAN
Trade Paper
ISBN 978-1-931847-66-7

Real-life stories from teachers who share their passion for shaping the lives of young people today

Mind, Heart, and Spirit: Educators Speak is a collection of real-life stories from a diverse group of educators on a wide range of issues such as how to deal with difficult students, the role of parents and religion in a child's education, and the similarities and differences in educating children in different cultures across the globe. Filled with interesting anecdotes and personal accounts, this is an intimate, sometimes frustrating, sometimes exhilarating insight into the experiences of all these educators as they have struggled to overcome various challenges in educating children. Their passion for teaching and their devotion to their students come shining through and offer a glimpse of the important role that Bahá'í education—with its emphasis on unity, tolerance, and diversity—can play in shaping the lives of young people today.

MARRIAGE
A FORTRESS FOR WELL-BEING

Bahá'í Publishing
$15.00 US / $17.00 CAN
Trade Paper
ISBN 978-1-931847-63-6

Valuable insight about applying spiritual principles to the practical realities of the marital relationship

Marriage: A Fortress for Well-Being offers valuable insight for every couple, whether married or in preparation for marriage, to apply spiritual principles to everyday needs. Redefining marriage as the basic building block for world peace and unity, the book explores issues such as dating, how to prepare for marriage, the purpose of marriage, conflict resolution, interracial marriage, raising children, divorce, and more. By taking an in-depth look at what the Bahá'í writings say about marriage, the book examines the institution in light of God's purpose for humanity and provides guidance for building spiritually founded marital unions. Coming at a time when modern social conditions are forcing a reexamination of the institution of marriage, the book offers sound advice, encouragement, and tremendous hope for the future. This new edition has a foreword by Elizabeth Marquardt, author of *Between Two Worlds: The Inner Lives of Children of Divorce,* and an affiliate scholar at the Institute for American Values.